IN THE PUBLIC INTEREST?

ASSESSING THE POTENTIAL OF PUBLIC INTEREST COMPANIES

Paul Maltby

30-32 Southampton Street, London WC2E 7RA
Tel: 020 7470 6100 Fax: 020 7470 6111
info@ippr.org.uk
www.ippr.org
Registered charity 800065

The Institute for Public Policy Research (ippr), established in 1988, is Britain's leading independent think tank on the centre left. The values that drive our work include delivering social justice, deepening democracy, increasing environmental sustainability and enhancing human rights. Through our well-researched and clearly argued policy analysis, our publications, our media events, our strong networks in government, academia and the corporate and voluntary sector, we play a vital role in maintaining the momentum of progressive thought.

ippr's aim is to bridge the political divide between the social democratic and liberal traditions, the intellectual divide between the academics and the policy makers and the cultural divide between the policy-making establishment and the citizen. As an independent institute, we have the freedom to determine our research agenda. ippr has charitable status and is funded by a mixture of corporate, charitable, trade union and individual donations.

Research is ongoing, and new projects being developed, in a wide range of policy areas including sustainability, health and social care, social policy, citizenship and governance, education, economics, democracy and community, media and digital society and public private partnerships. We will shortly embark on major new projects in the fields of public service reform, overseas development and democratic renewal. In 2003 we aim to grow into a permanent centre for contemporary progressive thought, recognised both at home and globally.

For further information you can contact ippr's external affairs department on info@ippr.org, you can view our website at www.ippr.org and you can buy our books from Central Books on 0845 458 9910 or email ippr@centralbooks.com.

Production & design by **EMPHASIS**
ISBN 1 86030 217 3
© IPPR 2003

Contents

Acknowledgements

IPPR is grateful to the Housing Corporation, the Royal Bank of Canada, Abbey National and the Places for People group for their generous support of this project.

I would like to thank all those who contributed ideas to the report. I would particularly like to thank those who wrote papers or gave presentations for seminars, including the PricewaterhouseCoopers Corporate Finance team, Adrian Bell and Duncan McCallum at the Royal Bank of Canada, Adrian Montague, Chris Gibson-Smith, Alan Murie at CURS, Ed Mayo at the New Economics Foundation, Christine Whitehead at the LSE, Peter Impey at Partnerships UK, and Stephen Duckworth. Thanks also to Ian Keys at Pinnacle PSG, Mike Gerrard and James Papps at Partnerships UK, and others in government departments and elsewhere who commented on the text.

This report could not have been written without the help of Peter Robinson, senior economist at the IPPR, and many others at the institute including Tony Grayling and Liz Kendall.

Although IPPR has benefited from assistance from many quarters, the views expressed in the book are the responsibility of the author alone.

About the author

Paul Maltby is IPPR's research fellow in public private partnerships. He was previously Environment, Transport and Regions Policy Officer in the Labour Party's policy unit.

Preface

It is now nearly two years since IPPR published our major report *Building Better Partnerships* which set the tone for the debate about public private partnerships in the UK. The policy on public service reform has moved on since then, but PPPs remain a huge source of contention.

In 1997 the new Labour Government was concerned about the quality of public infrastructure, and particularly with the sorry state of many schools and hospitals. The Private Finance Initiative (PFI) was seen as a way to end endemic cost and time overruns and to help ensure the quality of assets throughout their lifetime.

By the time of the 2001 general election it was not the quality of public buildings that was exercising the electorate, it was the quality of the services that went on inside those assets. The Government's attention shifted away from infrastructure and towards the much trickier issue of public service reform.

The Government has been keen to demonstrate its continued appetite for organisational reform to help in this process of change. The PFI is developing into a more service-orientated policy. For example all staff in the new NHS Diagnostic and Treatment Centres come under the scope of the private sector, not just ancillary workers such as cleaners and maintenance staff as was the case with previous PFIs in the health service.

However, the basic PFI model is dependent on building or maintaining assets, which restricts its use. In addition, commentators are also becoming conscious of the limits of contracting to a shareholder-owned company when delivering complex public services. A response has been the development of NHS foundation trusts.

In utility policy too, there is continuing debate about the best organisational form to deliver monopoly essential services. The Railtrack debacle focussed the minds of policy makers about the suitability of privatised shareholder-owned companies operating in the absence of competitive pressures. The furore surrounding the creation of Network Rail may have hastened the departure of a senior Cabinet Minister, but helped demonstrate that alternatives to both nationalisation and privatisation are possible.

The use of hybrid organisational forms such as the Public Interest Company is never easy. They are attacked by the political left and the right as departures from the accepted norm. Whilst this report makes no excuses for Public Interest Companies and indeed draws attention to their potential weaknesses, it holds out the possibility that using alternative organisational forms can and should play a role in public service reform. As with other types of public private partnerships, policy needs to be developed on the basis of rational understanding, not on dogma or ignorance.

Matthew Taylor
Director

Executive summary

This report explores the potential role of Public Interest Companies (PICs) in the delivery of UK public services.

There is currently a lively debate about how to reform public services. Levels of funding may often have a greater influence on service quality than the type of organisation used to deliver services. However, the basic organisational form of a public service can also play an important role.

The concept of the Public Interest Company is being increasingly considered in public service reform. Examples of PICs that already exist include Network Rail, National Air Traffic Services, the Welsh water company Glas Cymru and housing associations. Other PICs in the pipeline include the soon-to-be-created NHS foundation trusts. To date there has been little analysis of the advantages and disadvantages of the Public Interest Company model, and when it should be applied.

This report is written from a perspective of sympathetic scepticism about PICs. It considers that in the search for better quality and more responsive public services government should have at its disposal a full range of organisational forms. Private companies, various types of public private partnership – including Public Interest Companies – and state run organisations all have their place. However, as argued in previous IPPR reports on public private partnerships, the use of these various organisational forms should be informed by practical possibilities and results, not assumptions and dogma.

Definition

IPPR has used the term Public Interest Company to describe organisations which

- do not usually have shareholders

- are legally independent from the state

- deliver a public service

Whilst some PICs do have shareholders, these shareholders are restricted in their ability to profit from the organisation, or have another key interest in the organisation besides profit.

There is no one agreed definition of PICs, and others prefer alternative terms such as 'non profit distributing organisations'. There is also no one type of Public Interest Company; PICs are constituted in a variety of different forms and used for a variety of different purposes. PICs are frequently incorporated as Companies Limited by Guarantee, or as Industrial and Provident Societies. They can be Public or Private Limited Companies owned by users of a service or by government. They can also be specially constituted organisations or trusts.

The Government is currently considering whether to legislate to provide a new type of organisation suitable for PICs, a Community Interest Company. It is not clear that creating a new form for Public Interest Companies is necessary. Whilst a Community Interest Company could help prevent the (largely theoretical) possibility that a PIC might demutualise and lose its assets, amending existing company formats is an alternative and potentially less complex solution.

In addition to their form of legal incorporation, many PICs are also charities. Debates about Public Interest Companies have much in common with current discussions about encouraging greater involvement of the voluntary sector in the delivery of public services. Whilst this report considers the relationship between the voluntary sector and PICs, it does not attempt a detailed discussion of this wider issue.

Potential benefits of PICs

Although likely to face practical problems, Public Interest Companies have the potential to play an important role in the delivery of public services. There are four key areas where their use may be appropriate:

- When contracting for complex public services where the public interest or issues such as safety are key, and where the usual reliance on a contract alone is unlikely to be enough to secure the public interest (for example, NHS foundation trusts).

- For local regeneration schemes or other areas of the public services where the key policy aim is to improve social capital and promote a greater involvement of the public in a particular service (for example, development trusts).

- For monopoly essential services where users are able to play an important governance role (for example, air traffic control and electricity distribution).

- For services where there is a significant element of public subsidy, such as public transport. Where a service has both monopoly elements and high levels of public subsidy the case might be particularly strong (for example, Network Rail).

Potential difficulties

Whilst PICs may be a useful organisational form for some public services, they are no panacea. Their use requires caution in two complex areas: corporate governance and dealing with financial risk. These are the roles usually carried out by shareholders in a typical private company.

Governance and accountability

The absence of shareholders in Public Interest Companies means they require alternative methods of corporate governance. PICs that have access to private finance should not presume that lenders will carry out this role in place of shareholders. Many PICs rely on appointed 'members', who might be selected from stakeholder groups such as service users, the wider community, staff, financiers, and the government.

Some see the stakeholder governance possible in PICs as their principle attraction, since this enables PICs to involve local users and staff. PICs might improve the public's sense of 'ownership' over services. Meanwhile, in certain cirumstances, PICs organised as Consumer Service Corporations can provide better governance than might be expected from pension funds and other institutional shareholders. However, not all PICs will have an adequate pool of interested stakeholders who are willing or able to provide effective governance. There are also dangers that in some services stakeholders will have divergent views which will prevent them being able to present company directors with a clear set of priorities. Whilst stakeholder governance can provide advantages, these advantages should not be presumed to follow automatically from the model. The composition and effectiveness of governing bodies will be critical for PICs and should be thought through carefully.

Finance and risk

As with other public private partnerships such as the Private Finance Initiative, there is a temptation on the part of government to use PICs in order to move government spending from the government's accounts. For PICs supported by taxation alone this is little more than an 'off balance sheet' accounting trick and using them for this reason should be resisted. Alternatives to private finance, such as the prudential borrowing frameworks currently being developed for local government, might be more applicable.

For PICs that do continue to use private finance, serious attention should be paid as to how these organisations will deal with financial risk. This report identifies six ways in which risk can be dealt with without relying on shareholders, although in general these methods are less effective. PICs may therefore be more suitable to relatively low risk ventures.

PICs that use private finance rely on debt (such as bonds or bank loans) rather than on the mixture of debt and equity (such as shares) found in typical companies. Because debt is typically cheaper than equity, some commentators claim this means PICs have access to lower costs of borrowing. This is true in some unusual circumstances, but generally the overall costs of finance for PICs will be the same as for typically financed companies.

Conclusion

Public Interest Companies are already being used across a range of public services for a variety of reasons, and new uses of the model are in development. Generalisations about when and where they should be used or avoided in the future are problematic: recommendations really need to be made on a case by case basis. However, there are some areas where PICs could be used to good effect.

Two examples are the new NHS foundation trusts and various social enterprises set up to help regenerate local communities. The success of the public interest company air traffic control organisation in Canada,

Nav Canada, leads us to recommend a similar structure for National Air Traffic Services.

There are other areas where the use of PICs might offer an alternative to current policy, but where the case for change is less clear cut. Examples might include the use of PICs in electricity distribution, as a vehicle for British Energy, or as an alternative to the few remaining local authority bus companies.

There are other areas where analysis suggests the use of PICs owes more to political expediency than sound policy principles. For example, the proposed 'not-for-profit PFIs' might bring some welcome diversity into the PFI market but are unlikely to result in the radical change their label suggests.

As interest in PICs becomes more widespread, the Government should keep a level head. It should be realistic about the potential of PICs to improve public involvement and accountability, and they should be cautious about financial justifications for PICs. One of the greatest dangers to the success of PICs would be for them to become a new policy fad, applied without due consideration of their suitability.

PICs are already used to deliver some successful key public services. The evidence from this experience suggests that their use is complex and has some drawbacks as well as advantages. However, PICs should be routinely considered as an option alongside other alternative structures. Reform of the public services is likely to remain near the top of the political agenda for the foreseeable future and PICs should play their proper part in this process.

1. Contexts

Introduction

In 2001 and 2002 a new term, the 'Public Interest Company' (PIC) entered the policy lexicon. The PIC has been at the forefront of the debate over the future of public services.

For example, Stephen Byers MP, the then Secretary of State for Transport announced his intention to replace Railtrack, the failing privatised rail infrastructure company with Network Rail, a 'Company Limited by Guarantee' (Byers 2001). Alan Milburn, Secretary of State for health proposed the creation of 'NHS foundation trusts' as a way in which top performing hospitals could gain more independence from Whitehall (Milburn 2002). And the private partners in the public private partnership for National Air Traffic Services (NATS) announced their involvement in the project would be 'not for commercial return' (NATS 2001).

Meanwhile, away from the spotlight of central government, the Welsh Water company Glas Cymru published successful first year results (Glas Cymru 2002). The London Borough of Hackney decided their local education authority would be better run by a not-for-profit trust at arms length from their own political control (Hackney Borough Council 2001). And in neighbouring Tower Hamlets the council began to put in place a new procurement regime to increase the amount of services delivered by charities and other community organisations (*East End Life* 2002).

These examples all feature organisations delivering public services, which are legally independent from government, but which do not have shareholders. In short they are all Public Interest Companies. Not all have described themselves as such. In fact a number of terms have been used to describe these particular types of organisations including 'not-for-profits', 'not-for-profit distributing organisations', 'mutuals', 'social enterprises', and 'non-profits'. Slowly, however, the term 'Public Interest Company' is being used to denote these organisations of vastly different size and purpose; although some have used the term in a more specific way to signify a new type of legal entity similar to the proposed Community Interest Company (see pages 10-13).

To date there has been no generic assessment of PICs, and only limited discussion of them within the context of other types of public private partnership (IPPR 2001). IPPR and other organisations such as the Social Market Foundation have discussed their potential in specific circumstances, such as the rail and water industries (Grayling 2002; Stones 2001). However, there is little understanding about what these organisations can offer across the range of public services.

Government does not appear to have a coherent view about Public Interest Companies. The Department of Health is enthusiastic about the model in the form of NHS foundation trusts, whilst the Treasury has appeared more cautious. Others, such as the Department for Transport display a schizophrenic attitude: the Department strongly opposed London Mayor Ken Livingstone's PIC proposal for the London Underground, but put in place a PIC-like compromise for National Air Traffic Services (NATS), and made a pioneering use of a Public Interest Company for Network Rail. Curiously, Public Interest Companies appear to be favoured more in Scotland where traditionally public private partnerships have faced significant political opposition.

Politics figures highly in any debate about PICs, for good reason. The debate on PICs is entering unchartered territory in the public services. It is central to discussions surrounding structural reform of much loved public services such as the National Health Service. Also, as a hybrid organisation it slips between easy definitions of what is public and what is private, challenging entrenched political attitudes of both left and right. PICs are bound to be controversial.

This report is an attempt to offer a non-partisan, hard-headed and comprehensive explanation and evaluation of Public Interest Companies. It explains what PICs are and the wide range of ways in which they can be constituted. It addresses the question of whether government should legislate for a new legal form. It examines whether PICs can provide effective governance and accountability, which is a key issue of contention between supporters and detractors of the model. It also addresses crucial issues about finance and risk, which go to the heart of arguments for and against the concept; addressing questions such as can PICs borrow more cheaply than typical companies, should borrowing remain on the Government's balance sheet; what happens when PICs go bust; and how do you deal with risk in the absence of shareholders? Throughout there are case studies of PICs and evaluations of how and why they are used.

IPPR has led the debate on Public Private Partnerships since early 1999 when the Commission on Public Private Partnerships was established. This Commission resulted in the key publication Building Better Partnerships (IPPR 2001). This document follows in its wake. It takes a similarly pragmatic approach; we do not believe one should – or in fact can – take an ideological view about whether public, private or hybrid formats will deliver the best policy solution before looking at the context.

Whilst the report is based on a presumption in favour of best value in public services (that is, services of the highest quality delivered at the lowest cost), it is important to emphasise that IPPR is not neutral about political choices or about what our public services should achieve. As a centre-left organisation we want to see high quality public services. Changing organisational form may or may not help achieve this. Indeed, issues such as the appropriate organisational form for a service are often secondary to debates about what the appropriate level of funding should be to support the public services. Whilst the choice of the appropriate body to deliver public services may no longer be determined by ideology, questions about the type and level of services will remain central to the party political debate.

This publication will argue that there is a proper place for Public Interest Companies in some of our public services. However, it emphasises that these organisations are not a panacea. On the contrary, PICs are frequently problematic, especially in issues such as finance and governance. These problems might not be insurmountable but they need honesty and sensitivity on the part of government to ensure success. This report is not evangelical about the PIC concept, it is more of a critical friend.

Definition

Public Interest Companies could be said to have three defining factors. They:

- do not usually have shareholders. Where they do have shareholders they are restricted in their ability to profit from the organisation, or they have another key interest in the organisation besides profit.

- are legally independent from the state.

- deliver a public service.

Even though Public Interest Companies are sometimes referred to as 'not-for-profits', such a term is misleading. Managers of PICs will typically want to make a financial surplus in order to remain stable, viable bodies. The difference from private companies is that these surpluses are theoretically all reinvested in the organisation and there are no dividends paid to external shareholders. It would be wrong to presume that no one will make money from PICs, they invariably will. In many ways there is little practical difference between PICs making surpluses that are distributed to staff and private companies making profits that they distribute to both staff and shareholders. PICs are not anti-business organisations. Rather, they are a different type of organisation: a hybrid between the public and private sectors.

The voluntary sector

There is an established academic literature that includes formal definitions of the non-profit sector. The 'non-profit sector' is used interchangeably with what is often referred to as the charitable sector; it is not necessarily concerned with delivering public services and it emphasises voluntary contributions.[1] It is a different type of organisation from that being discussed in this publication.

Although the definition of PICs used in this report does not include a voluntary element, this is not to downplay the importance of the charitable sector within not-for-profit service delivery. The voluntary element is an important, but not sufficient criteria for determining Public Interest Company status.

Debate about PICs has considerable overlaps with current discussions regarding the potential role of the voluntary sector in delivering public services. The Treasury held a cross-cutting review looking at the role of the voluntary sector in public services which concluded in Autumn 2002 (HM Treasury 2002a; NCVO 2002), and the Active Community Unit in the Home Office is also looking to increase public involvement in voluntary services. The Unit has a Public Service Agreement target to increase voluntary activity by five per cent between 2002 and 2006 (HM Treasury 2002b) and also has a new

£125 million *Futurebuilders* fund to help increase voluntary sector delivery of public services. PICs may play an important role in achieving this target.

There is already a considerable degree of voluntary sector provision of public services. This includes larger organisations such as Turning Point, which provides services to those suffering from drug and alcohol misuse. There are also many smaller community enterprises and charities that carry out more local level activities. IPPR has been working with the Improvement and Development Agency and the New Economics Foundation to put in place a new procurement regime for Tower Hamlets Borough Council in London in order to increase the level of voluntary sector provision of services. Tower Hamlets Council is keen to use such organisations in order to help make contact with hard-to-reach groups such as the seriously disadvantaged and those from minority ethnic groups which are difficult for the Council to reach through normal delivery mechanisms.

Although there are some fascinating issues currently being worked on with respect to the voluntary sector and public service delivery, this report aims to take a more general view of Public Interest Companies. As a result it does not dwell on the significant and complex debate about the particular role of the voluntary sector within public services.

The public service continua

Before looking at the choices available to public service managers it is important to make the distinction between two types of public services; the revenue generating public enterprises and the more general tax-funded public services.

The public enterprises are characterised by user charges, and have typically been the focus of privatisations or PPPs. Where they remain in the public sector they have often been granted more organisational independence than other forms of public services. Examples include most of the privatised utilities, the Post Office, most public transport services and leisure services. The existence of identifiable user charges means the public enterprises have had a more obvious route into private finance than other services wholly reliant on government funding.

The more general tax-funded public services consist of core state services such as the majority of services provided by the NHS, and all schooling up to the age of 18. Even under the Conservative government in the 1980s and 1990s the general public services remained largely delivered by the state itself. There was some movement away from direct government provision, for example, the setting up of quasi-autonomous NHS trusts. In addition, some private provision, for example of pharmacy services, became an accepted feature of the public service landscape. However, a widening of private sector involvement in the core public services remained highly contentious.

Public Interest Companies are only one of a range of organisational options available to public services managers. These options range from full public sector control, through to complete privatisation. This could be expressed in a simplified manner through two 'public service continua' shown in Figures 1.1 and 1.2.

Figure 1.1 The public enterprise continuum

state-owned industries	for-profit PPPs	private companies
PUBLIC SECTOR		PRIVATE SECTOR
PICs	regulated privatised companies	

Figure 1.2 The general public services continuum

state-provided services	PICs	joint ventures	private services
PUBLIC SECTOR			PRIVATE SECTOR
quangos	contracts with PICs	contracts with for-profit companies	

Whilst this report will necessarily involve some discussion of these other organisations that deliver public services, the priority will be to define and describe the various types of Public Interest Company.

Other types of services outside the public sector continua

The majority of PICs could be expected to deliver typical public services to the general public, as public enterprises or general taxpayer-funded public services. However, there are a number of other types of services that are, or could be, delivered using Public Interest Company structures:

- commissioning bodies

  PICs can be used as a structure not just for service delivery organisations, but also for the organisations involved in procuring those services. An example is the Primary Care Trusts which have recently been established to commission health care from the NHS trusts on behalf of patients. The Department of Health has said it is considering PIC status for these bodies (see Case Study 5, p52 on NHS Foundation Trusts)

- funding intermediaries

  Education Capital Finance PLC and the Housing Finance Corporation are both examples of PICs that do not deliver or procure services, but which nevertheless provide an important public service. These so-called 'funding intermediaries' were established in order to develop the private sector market in financing other PICs, such as further education colleges and housing associations.

Classification

There is no one type of Public Interest Company. Instead there are a multiplicity of organisational forms that could usefully be described as PICs. The type of service provided by PICs ranges from large utilities such as Network Rail, through organisations such as City Academies (new legally independent state schools), to small-scale regeneration bodies. Despite the attention they have recently received, the idea behind PICs is far from new; housing associations have been operating public services in this way for well over a century.

Before discussing various structural forms of Public Interest Companies it is useful to understand how 'typical' companies are organised. 'Typical' companies are usually either Private Limited Companies ('limited companies', indicated by the letters 'Ltd'), where shares are owned by private individuals or other organisations and are not sold on open markets; or Public Limited Companies (PLCs) where shares *can* be bought or sold on public stock exchanges. Typical companies (and Companies Limited by Guarantee, a form often used by

PICs) are registered at Companies House, the Government organisation that holds records on companies and their directors.[2]

Figure 1.1 Organisational forms of Public Interest Companies		
Type of PIC	*Details*	*Evaluation*
Companies limited by guarantee	These companies are answerable to members rather than shareholders. They are a common legal structure of PICs. Members carry out the same functions as shareholders in a typical company, but they are appointed to the role and do not have a direct financial stake in the company. Members might consist of government representatives, service users, trade unions, independent experts and financiers. Companies limited by guarantee can vary significantly in their size, purpose and format. Examples include Glas Cymru (the Welsh water utility), a number of Housing Associations transferred from local authority control, The Learning Trust (the PIC that has taken over the Local Education Authority functions of Hackney Borough Council), and Network Rail (the organisation that has replaced Railtrack). Most Development Trusts (local community-based regeneration organisations) are also incorporated as Companies limited by guarantee.	An advantage of Companies limited by guarantee is that they are registered at Companies House and regulated under the Companies Act. This means they share the same high quality case law (legal history which affects the organisations) as typical companies. This makes them a modern and flexible choice for PICs.
Industrial and Provident Societies (IPS)	Often referred to as 'mutuals' or 'co-ops', there are two main types of Industrial and Provident Societies. The first is the bona fide mutual, owned by its members for its members. The second is the 'benefit of the community society', a mutual that provides services for people other than just its members. Members own the organisation with each usually owning one share which cannot be traded or transferred, and which provides no rights to interest, dividend or bonus. Examples of IPS PICs include Greenwich leisure, which runs ex-local authority leisure services in the London borough, and the majority of non-transfer Housing Associations. BUPA is an interesting example of a provident society; until recently BUPA provided only private health services, although it now delivers some public health services under contract to the NHS.	A disadvantage of IPSs is the amount of additional regulations. For example, an organisation needs to prove to the regulator (the Financial Services Authority) why it needs to be an IPS rather than another type of company. IPSs also have their own case law, which is less well developed than that for typical companies.

Private or public limited companies owned by users of a service	If a limited company or a PLC is owned by the users of the service then the owners clearly have a different relationship to the company than would typical shareholders. This allows them to be classed as PICs. Many would also be considered to be Consumer Service Corporations, a sub-category of PICs. An example of a PLC PIC is the joint venture PPP for National Air Traffic Services (NATS) which is owned by the Government, staff, and a consortium of airline companies. These shareholders have indicated that they consider their ownership to be on a 'not for commercial return' basis.	Although this format offers all the flexibilities and freedoms of a typical company, it is difficult to ensure the 'not-for-profit' aspect of the PIC. For example, the shareholders in NATS have said they will operate on a 'not for commercial return' basis, but this is viewed with some suspicion by users not involved in governance.
Public or private limited company, wholly owned by the Government	The Post Office and BNFL are both examples of public corporations transferred to a company, but which are owned entirely by the Government. The Post Office is a private limited company, whilst BNFL is a public limited company. In the case of BNFL, the Government has indicated that it would like to see a minority stake eventually sold to the private sector. Local authority owned airports and few remaining council-owned bus companies are organised in this way. For example, the Manchester Airport Group of Companies is owned by Manchester City Council (55%) and the other nine Greater Manchester District Councils (5% each).	This type of PIC is a well-understood compromise between nationalisation and privatisation for public enterprises. It often indicates that Government would like to fully privatise the service in the future. A potential downside is that the Government can find it difficult to be an effective shareholder and give clear objectives to managers.
Share trusts	An example is Education Capital Finance, the funding intermediary for the further education sector. It is classed as a PIC because it is a private limited company but its nominal share capital is held in trust. This PIC is a holding company which in turn owns 100% of the operating company organised as a typical PLC. The trust is established in favour of a not-for-profit or charitable purpose, and independent trustees are obliged to act in accordance with these instructions.	This model provides significant freedoms for managers, but brings with it the potential for lax accountability. Institutional charitable trustees are unlikely to have an incentive to act as strong shareholders, and in any case have only indirect shareholder powers through the holding company.

Trusts and special organisations	There are a number of bodies that do not use existing company models, but which are specially created organisations that conform to PIC definitions. This category includes public trusts such as the Trust Ports. An example is the Port of London Authority which was created in 1908 with the capacity to issue its own bonds, secured by port revenues. Most of the Universities set up before 1992 could also be placed under this classification. A small number were set up by their own Act of Parliament, but most were established by a royal charter granted through the Privy Council, together with an associated set of statutes. This form of organisation is known as a chartered corporation.	These types of organisations are quite rare. Although the model can be molded to the precise purpose envisaged, they can take up unnecessarily legislative time and effort.
Charity	Charitable status is not in itself a form of incorporation; it is granted in addition to an organisation's basic legal status. Charities are usually organised as either companies, trusts, or they are unincorporated or 'exempt' (ie incorporated as Industrial and Provident Societies, by Royal Charter, or otherwise by statute). Organisations which are well known for being charities deliver many public services, especially in areas such as personal social services, hospice care and home/school links.	Charitable status confers particular benefits onto an organisation, for example tax exemptions. However, in exchange charitable status also confers certain restrictions, including strict rules on trading and on trustees receiving benefits. They are heavily regulated by the Charity Commission which ensures they operate in the public interest.

The case for a new legal form: the Community Interest Company

The Prime Minister's Strategy Unit has followed a number of pressure groups in suggesting a new type of legal organisation to incorporate Public Interest Companies. The Strategy Unit have called this new body a 'Community Interest Company' (Strategy Unit 2002).

There are two main arguments for such a move; that it could deal with the possibility of demutualisation and that it could help make the sector more visible and understandable to financiers and the public.

Demutualisation is a potential problem for PICs. As many of the mutual building societies discovered in the last decade, it is possible for members of an Industrial and Provident Society to vote to turn their organisation into a shareholder-owned company. The same is true for Companies Limited by Guarantee and other PIC formats. Arguably, it was not a major concern of the Government to prevent building society demutualisations as they did not provide a key public service. However, if the Government is considering transferring public services from public institutions to PICs, they need to pay attention to the demutualisation problem. Quite rightly, government would be worried if members of a foundation trusts or Network Rail transferred the assets to the private sector without their approval.

Creating a new legal form is not the only solution to this problem. PICs can create (or change) their rules to make demutualisation a highly unlikely scenario. For example, Standard Life, the mutual financial services company and Europe's biggest mutual, changed its rules in March 2002 so that the number of signatures needed to call a special general meeting of the society where demutualisation could be discussed rose from 50 to 1,000. It also raised the number of members required to nominate a director from two to 250 (Standard Life 2002). In addition, newly formed Public Interest Companies can protect their not-for-profit status by using their memorandum and articles of association. For example, clauses four and five of Glas Cymru's articles of association state that members shall not benefit financially from the organisation and clause six of the articles of association prevent any subsequent changes to these clauses.[3]

The Government could amend the existing Company's Act and other relevant PIC legislation to help prevent demutualisations. Gareth R Thomas MP's Industrial and Provident Societies Act 2002 aimed to do just that for this group most at risk from demutualisation. The Act places co-operatives registered under the industrial and provident societies legislation in the same position as building societies by ensuring there is substantial democratic participation on decisions on whether or not to convert to a company. It states that demutualisation can only take place on a 50 per cent turnout and the 75 per cent vote in favour, mirroring the existing provision in building society law. Similarly, Mark Todd MP's Co-operatives and Community Benefit Societies Bill, which received its second reading on 31 January 2003, aims to permit community benefit societies to safeguard their assets in perpetuity.

The second justification for a new legal form is that the current choice of organisational forms for PICs can lead to confusion. The suggestion is that a new legal form would help bring awareness to social entrepreneurs, public managers, financiers and the general public of this 'new' hybrid organisational form. The Public Interest Company group of charity lawyers have argued that a new legal form would not only improve awareness, but could also reduce the complexity and legal costs of establishing a PIC (Lloyd 2001).

The perception of PICs by financiers can also be a problem. They are often grouped together with charities and seen as a poor investment. It is undoubtedly the case that a clash of cultures does account for some of the difficulties that Public Interest Companies have in attracting finance. However, PICs need to address difficult issues such as their frequent lack of collateral and secure income streams before all the blame can be attributed to the banks. Until these difficult issues are addressed by PICs, providing an additional organisational form is likely to prove only a cosmetic solution.

It has also been suggested that improving the marketability of PICs relies on emphasising their public benefit. There is an understandable enthusiasm in attempting to replicate the high levels of public support that charities receive. However, if the aim is to produce a legal form that is held in the same degree of public affection as charities then there is a need to face up to the trade off between protecting that status and the necessary regulation that it must involve. Charities are a tightly regulated group of organisations, and this has been at the root of their success since the first Charity Law in 1601. Proposals for a new legal form put forward by the Strategy Unit make it clear that they see the 'public interest' element of these organisations as being regulated at the point of registration.

However, it is unclear whether managers and social entrepreneurs would relish the opportunity to submit themselves to greater regulation in exchange for the good of the wider Public Interest Company movement. Unlike charities, there will be no automatic tax benefit in becoming such an organisation. There is a possibility that if such a new legal form came into being along these lines then it might be shunned in favour of the many existing forms of incorporation; some of which already have as many freedoms as typical private sector companies.

Overall, the case for a new legal form for Public Interest Companies is far from conclusive. The multiplicity of legal forms available for Public Interest Companies could be seen as an advantage – enabling PICs to be applied in a wide variety of circumstances – not a hindrance. The Government should act on the issue of demutualisation, and if a new legal form achieves this then it will not have been in vain. However, it should be wary of being over-prescriptive; too much regulation to determine the public benefit, or a specification about the degree of public involvement in governance could make any new legal form less attractive than existing alternatives. Either way, legislating for a 'community interest company' is unlikely to bring about any radical change in the use of PICs as envisaged by some supporters.

Case Study 1: PICs and schools

There are three potential uses of Public Interest Companies in compulsory education; in the organisation of the schools themselves, for school subsidiary companies, and to take on the roles of Local Education Authorities.

Most typical state schools are not dissimilar from Public Interest Companies. Although Local Education Authorities (LEAs) have a significant influence over schools, others such as teachers, parents and representatives of the local community are also involved in school governance. In addition, headteachers have a fair degree of managerial independence and elected officials do not directly vet their decisions.

This quasi-PIC format has been taken one step further with new state schools which are legally independent and have a degree of managerial independence from LEAs. New 'City Academies' are actually incorporated as Companies Limited by Guarantee.

The recent development of school companies offers another potential for the use of PICs within a schooling environment. The 1998 School Standards and Frameworks Act permitted individual schools to establish subsidiary companies, and the 2002 Education Act seeks to extend this principle to allow groups of schools to set up joint companies.

A key driver behind these school companies is to enable the development of a school-to-school market, whereby schools with particular skills in a certain area can sell these skills to other schools (Hallgarten 2003).

● **Thomas Telford CTC in Shropshire** has been developing ICT-based GCSE and GNVQ courses for over five years, which are now used by over five hundred schools. About twenty people work on the materials, four of which are full time. All of the creation, marketing and distribution is carried out in house. The profits (which have been estimated at £4 million) are, according to Headteacher Kevin Satchwell, used 'to oil the mechanisms of sharing'. They have sponsored a City Academy in Walsall, and supported many specialist schools and Primary projects.

- **Varndean School in Brighton** is a mixed 11-16 community comprehensive with Technology College Status. It has developed three sources of income generation: First, Varndean e-learning sells software and after-sales support to schools and colleges. Established at the school in 2001 by ex-staff, it profit shares with the school based on royalties. It grossed £400,000 profit in the first year of trading. Software is given free to other Brighton and Hove schools. ICT Technical Support and Consultancy is offered to schools and colleges, as is Investors in People Consultancy.

The school-to-school market is not only intended to facilitate the best use of specialist skills throughout the school system, but is intended as a staff development tool, providing quality teachers with an incentive to develop. However, individual school companies can be used for other purposes, for example, **Greensward School in Essex** has built and manages an on-site fitness centre open to the public.

Although the joint companies proposed in the 2002 Education Bill could be used to develop the school-to-school market, their primary purpose is to enable the development of joint-procurement of goods by schools, taking forward the agenda of the Byatt report on local government procurement (Byatt 2001).

There is a surprising lack of regulation surrounding school companies. Schedule 10.3 of the School Standards and Frameworks Act 1998 allows governing bodies to 'do anything which appears to them to be necessary or expedient for the purposes of, or in connection with, the conduct of the school', which includes setting up a school company. These companies can be incorporated in any way, and there are no regulations surrounding their purpose or their governance. On the other hand current proposals surrounding *joint* school companies require approval for the formation of the companies from Local Education Authorities, who will retain a key governance role. There is also Department for Education and Skills guidance covering joint companies. The difference in required regulation between individual and joint school companies means it is unclear whether the new joint companies will be relatively attractive.

A key question is whether school companies could or should be constituted as Public Interest Companies. There are no restrictions preventing schools using company formats such as Companies Limited by Guarantee, so using a PIC-like structure is certainly possible.

A key consideration, as always with PICs, will be finance and risk. This will be a particular issue if the companies need to borrow money to make any initial investment. If these school companies borrow money, who will pay if things go wrong? If schools enter into joint ventures with typical shareholder-owned companies it may be that the company shareholders bear the risk in the project (this will mean they receive most financial rewards as well as pay up if things go wrong). This appears a sensible way to cope with risk in school companies, and may be the preferred option.

Using a PIC is possible; although banks, which are likely to be the principle source of finance for most of these companies, are highly unlikely to lend without some security. Schools need to be aware of this before they commit themselves, as it may mean that some school assets or budgets will need to be put at risk if lending is required. There are currently no regulations or guidelines concerning such issues. Given that schools are unlikely to be experienced in setting up companies and taking financial risks of this type government should set out some good practice in this area; perhaps suggesting the highest proportion of a school budget could be risked safely.

The school-to-school market is unlikely to develop without finance being made available, and it is not clear whether commercial companies will be interested in providing finance to the school sector. An alternative source of finance could be education venture capital, perhaps supplied by the new Schools Innovation Unit in the Department for Education and Skills. They could inject finance into schemes and bear the financial risks.

The PIC format might be attractive for school companies. It could certainly help avoid the sensitive issue of a private profit motive within the school environment, which might act as a barrier for joint ventures with the private sector in some schools. Schools could avoid any private profit motive by setting up private limited companies where the school held all the shares. However, private limited companies do not allow for stakeholder governance, which might be a key priority for schools wishing to promote interaction with parents or the local community. Parents are likely to be relatively effective governors given their close relationship to the school whilst their children attend; they certainly compare favourably to public members of NHS foundation trusts who will only experience hospital care infrequently. Moreover, including a range of staff in the governance of a school company might be desirable where staff development is a principle aim of the project.

The existence of school companies also allows for some innovative possibilities. For instance, parents might be persuaded to provide a small investment in a subsidiary school company designed to carry out ancillary functions. It could be formulated as an Industrial and Provident society, and then if the company then made any profits, investing parents might receive a low yield interest payment every year (which they could choose to reinvest in the school company). Doing this would provide the necessary risk capital which would facilitate private finance from banks. Providing parents with a financial stake in the activities of the school company might also aid parental interest in wider schooling activities. Such schemes would clearly be difficult to set up in deprived areas, although they may be an attractive concept for schools where parents were on modest incomes.

A third potential use of PICs in compulsory education is in taking on the role of the Local Education Authority. This has happened in the London Borough of Hackney, where a history of very poor management left the council to consider alternative methods of delivery. Hackney outsourced some elements of its education service to the *for-profit* company Nord Anglia in 1999, but the council decided to transfer the whole of the LEA to a stakeholder PIC called The Learning Trust in August 2002. *The Learning Trust* is contracted to the LEA and is judged on a number of performance indicators. The Board of Directors has members from outside the Trust including the Council, parents, governors as well as two head teachers who are non-executive directors. The former Chief Inspector of Schools in England, Mike Tomlinson, chairs the Trust.

Evidence of the extent of PICs and their performance

Most of the academic literature on 'nonprofits' relates to the charitable sector. There are no government statistics about the use or success of PICs. As a result there is little statistical information directly relevant to our study.

Regarding charities, the National Council for Voluntary Organisations estimated that £2.5 billion of general charities income (16 per cent of total income) is received as earned income from the UK Government (National Council for Voluntary Organisations 2002). Clearly, the charitable sector makes up only a proportion of all PIC activity.

There is also little data on the performance of most PICs in the UK. One exception is Jeremy Kendall's work at the London School of Economics on charitable provision of care for the elderly (Kendall 2000). His study made an attempt to judge the comparative efficiency and wider social outputs in various types of care for elderly people. Kendall found that the charitable and voluntary sector charged lower fees than for-profit providers in both residential and day care provision. However, these lower costs were attributed to a complex range of factors including the use of volunteers. The study also looked to non-resource outputs and found that there was evidence that the charitable sector was better than the for-profit sector at engaging residents in leisure and recreation pursuits. However, they found that in other respects there was little difference between them. Perhaps surprisingly, they found little evidence that manager's motivations differed between the for-profit and charitable sector, although it is worth noting that private care homes are typically small, family-run businesses, not large corporations.

There is some interesting academic material relating to Public Interest Company models of health provision in the US, although the evidence in this area is far from conclusive. For example, the American academics Norton and Staiger compared the volume of uninsured patients treated in for-profit and non-profit hospitals to determine whether ownership had an impact on the equity of services offered (Norton 1994). They found that when for-profit hospitals were located in the same area as non-profit hospitals they served an equivalent number of uninsured patients. However, they also found that for-profit hospitals indirectly avoided uninsured patients by locating in better-insured areas. The differences in the health systems between the UK and the USA mean that this study is not of direct relevance. However, it helps show the ways in which the private sector might seek to avoid unprofitable services whenever possible, even though day to day management decisions in PICs do not appear to offer a more publicly spirited regime.

Likewise, Mark Duggan has looked at how a hospital's type of ownership influences its response to profitable opportunities created by changes in US Government policy (Duggan 2000). He found that, perhaps contrary to expectations, that decision makers in private not-for-profit hospitals were just as responsive to financial incentives and were no more altruistic than their counterparts in profit-maximising facilities. Instead, he found that the soft budget constraint in publicly owned hospitals was the critical difference between behaviour in the three types of hospital. Druggan's study is intriguing. On one hand it shows that the presumed efficiencies of profit-maximising shareholder-based organisations over Public Interest Companies are somewhat illusory. On the other, it also demonstrates that the presumed ethical benefits of not-for-profit companies might also be contested.

2. The potential benefits of PICs

Contracting

Management freedoms

One of the main benefits of Public Interest Companies arises from a desire to provide public managers with clarity about what is expected of them, and to give them the freedoms they need to achieve those ends. Currently, many public sector managers, particularly those operating in the mainstream public services controlled from Whitehall have little clarity about their responsibilities. Managers of public services know that they will be heavily criticised by politicians, by the Public Accounts Committee, by the National Audit Office, or by the media if the decisions they take have negative results. However, managers also know that if those decisions result in success they will not be rewarded. In too many instances the result is a culture of risk aversion.

These problems have been dealt with in the past by both privatisations and through contracting for services. Privatisation makes some sense for public enterprises operating in competitive markets. But when applied to monopoly essential services such as water and rail infrastructure there have been some poor results (Kay 2001; Grayling 2002). Contracting for public services, particularly through public private partnerships, has been seen as a useful way to clarify desired outcomes in the public sector, as it asserts a much higher degree of public sector control over the service than occurs under a privatise and regulate model. This is one of the reasons behind the use of the Private Finance Initiative for public infrastructure projects. Although there have been mixed successes with the PFI, one of the main benefits has been that it has forced the public sector to clarify its desired outcomes and has inserted a previously unseen degree of management clarity in the delivery of the service. The private sector operator is then paid for the service it delivers according to the quality of that service over the lifetime of the contract (IPPR 2001).

Incomplete contracts

Whilst contracting might be an attractive way to provide clarity over what services need to be delivered, the necessarily incomplete nature of contracts can pose problems. For relatively simple public infrastructure and services that might be delivered through the Private Finance Initiative, such as new roads, it is relatively easy to specify all the important elements needed through a contract. If aspects of the contracts are unclear or if important elements have been left out, then the only downside is likely to be the cost of resolving the issue or renegotiating contracts.

However, for more complex projects decisions about what is and what is not included in a contract are critical. In mainstream public services, such as large NHS hospitals, there are an infinite number of small interactions that take place between staff and the public which take time and money, but which would not be considered priority outcomes or outputs. Such factors would be difficult to contract for, yet they are essential parts of these services. If a contract does not provide everything expected by the public sector, vital public interest issues will be at stake, not just cost considerations.

PICs offer an opportunity to provide a public sector safeguard when contracting for complex and vital public services. Because a range of stakeholders are in charge of corporate governance in the place of shareholders, PICs might be expected to behave differently from for-profit companies in a similar position. The profit maximising incentive of shareholders is diluted by the motives of other stakeholders. This can reduce the danger of incomplete contracts leading to the neglect of important social considerations.

Even when contracting for apparently relatively simple infrastructure PPPs where there is no face-to-face service delivery, the fear that the private sector might exploit the public interest for profit can lead to huge and complex contracts. The London Underground PPP is a good, if extreme, example. Although the contracts are not publicly available, Transport for London has revealed aspects of the contracts and performance regimes (Transport for London 2001). In it, there are a large number of complex formulas designed to determine performance standards. An example is the formula below, which is designed to test the 'ambience' or state of a train's environment.

$$TMS = \sum_j \left(\frac{QATAS_j \times W_j^T}{\sum_j W_j^T + \sum_k W_k^T} \right) + \sum_k \left(\frac{QATAS_k \times W_k^T}{\sum_j W_j^T + \sum_k W_k^T} \right)$$

It is difficult to draw conclusions from this formula without having access to the variables that it refers to. However, it helps demonstrate the vast array of inputs needed to determine the level of payments made to the private consortia. The level of bureaucracy needed for the private sector to carry out these calculations and for the public sector to verify them will be immense.

Is profit irreconcilable with the public interest?

It would be wrong to assume that these discussions about the usefulness of contracting to PICs rather than typical private companies means that there is an implication that distributing profits is irreconcilable with the delivery of public services. If a public service can be delivered to the same (or higher) standards, and the cost is the same (or lower) for taxpayers then there is a good case for using private sector companies to deliver those services. Indeed, the public sector has historically been overly cautious of the private sector, for example, the 'Ryrie rules' in place until 1992 constrained government departments from considering private sector solutions to public service problems. IPPR's report *Building Better Partnerships* (IPPR 2001) outlined various situations where a best value solution might be achieved through public private partnerships. There is also a case for saying that a best value solution can be achieved for public services using a privatise/regulate model in certain circumstances.

The key is to ensure that the degree of protection of the public interest is in proportion to the sensitivity of the public interest. For near-commercial services, such as telecommunications, regulation provides a light-touch protection of the public interest, but commercial competition also plays a significant role in protecting consumers. For areas where the public interest is more important contracts provide greater clarity about which services need to be delivered and the quality that is expected. Payments to the private companies should reflect their ability to meet these targets and the risks involved.

In situations where there are clear concerns over safety or other similar public concerns the profit maximising motive of a private sector contractor might be less appropriate than these alternatives. Such concerns are likely to be exacerbated for monopoly provision or for essential public services.

There may also be situations where a private sector solution injects a necessary degree of contestability into a public service, even when on balance the private sector solution does not appear most favourable. Contestability refers to the possibility that an under-performing public service institution could be replaced (either in whole, or just its management) by an alternative supplier. A good example is the prison sector, where the old monopoly of public service provision was shaken up and improved by the existence of a small number of prisons contracted in whole to the private sector (IPPR 2001).

It is right to avoid structuring public services in a way that encourages private companies to cut back on key public interest concerns. However, it is dangerous to presume a public sector solution, or indeed a PIC solution, will inherently deliver better quality public services.

Decentralisation

PICs can also be justified on the basis that they devolve power and responsibilities. The Government is not only becoming aware that it provides little clarity for some management roles, but that the 'command and control' model of public service delivery, where Whitehall effectively takes both management decisions and runs services directly, is looking increasingly shaky. There is precious little decentralisation of power to the front line or the local level in too many public services; a fact acknowledged by Gordon Brown, Chancellor of the Exchequer in a recent speech (Brown 2003), and by the Chancellor's Chief Economic Adviser, Ed Balls, in an introduction to a pamphlet for the New Local Government Network (Corry 2002).

The section on contracting above highlights how PICs can help this situation by providing a way in which complex public services can safely be delivered by devolved quasi-private sector organisations. But they can also help by allowing local organisations to set their own priorities, rather than just implementing a set of centrally imposed policy decisions. An example is the way in which service commissioning PICs could maintain a balance between the needs of central government, local government and the local community. Although the idea is still in development, Primary Care Trusts organised as PICs or 'foundations' could be seen in this way.

A PIC can also act as a service deliverer *and* have some control over its own priorities, which are in part dictated by stakeholders. Many PICs, including those delivering regeneration projects, come under this category.

If services are to be devolved, then the political responsibility for those decisions also needs to be devolved. Arguably one of the reasons why the NHS trusts failed to live up to their promised independence was that government ministers retained political responsibility. If Ministers know they will take the blame when things go wrong they will want to maintain a managerial influence. PICs need to devolve clear political accountability in addition to management authority if they are to be a useful tool in developing what has been termed by the New Local Government Network and some parts of government as 'the new localism' (Corry 2002).

The effect of subsidy

The source of income for a public service might be reflected in the type of structure used. This is a matter more of concern to the public enterprises which may be funded through a mix of user charges and government subsidies. The effect of subsidies does not arise for general public services because they are funded directly through taxation.

The public enterprises, though in part defined by their reliance on user fees, may also be dependent on direct Government subsidies. NATS has traditionally been able to cover all its costs through its income and was a net contributor to the public purse. Railtrack, on the other hand, was always heavily reliant upon public subsidy.

All other things being equal we could make a case that those enterprises not reliant on direct subsidy might be more suited to a regulated PLC model, and those that are heavily dependent on public subsidy might be more suited to hybrid models such as Public Interest Companies. Where a service has both monopoly elements and high levels of public subsidy the case might be particularly strong, for example for Network Rail (Corry 2003).

As seen with Railtrack and British Energy, shareholders can be adept at extracting additional subsidy from government. In addition, government is likely to want to retain some influence over how its funds are spent where there is significant subsidy. One of the reasons the PLC model did not work well for Railtrack was that shareholder pressure for higher profits favoured the extraction of additional subsidies from government rather than from achieving difficult efficiency gains from the core business. Despite the high levels of government subsidy and the fact that the rail network is a key national monopoly, the Government had little influence over how the rail network was run. This situation has changed considerably with the creation of Network Rail.

An option for monopoly enterprises

PICs can be used to run monopoly essential services reliant on user charges, as an alternative to either public ownership, or the more typical privatise/regulate model.

In this type of PIC – referred to as a Consumer Service Corporation– the users of the service can become in effect the owners, with key rights over governance (McCallum 2002). This aligns the interests of management and users and avoids the usual conflict between a monopoly corporation and its consumers, whereby the corporation wants to charge high rates and cut quality, and consumers want to pay low rates and receive high quality services. These types of PICs can achieve high overall efficiency and end the need for risky price regulation.

To work users need to be effective governors of the organisation. For example, users need to be a fairly cohesive group with similar aims. They should have similar views about the appropriate trade-off between, say, prices, investment and safety. Also, users need to have a strong interest in the organisation. The most effective driver is that the costs of the organisation should make a real difference to their day-to-day existence. Such an organisation will not work if users might end up with, say, a £1 increase on a £10 annual bill. It is more likely to work if there are sophisticated users – for example corporate users – who face significant risks if the costs of the organisation are allowed to spiral out of control. The Consumer Service Corporation is discussed in more detail on page 64.

Case study 2: Further Education

Public Interest Companies are found in two areas of the Further Education (FE) sector; both in the providers of FE, and in an intermediary funding body 'Education Capital Finance'.

The Further and Higher Education Act 1992 established FE colleges as legally independent 'further education corporations'. The Act removed them from Local Education Authority (LEA) control. FE colleges operate as Public Interest Companies, providing further and higher education in addition to various other education services. Between 85 per cent and 95 per cent of their funding comes from central government (most of it via the Learning and Skills Council), with the rest coming from student user fees and charges (Housing Finance Corporation 2002).

The Learning and Skills Council is responsible for all publicly-funded education and training, other than higher education. It both funds and plans activity in the further education sector. Although further education colleges are able to raise finance directly, they require the consent of the Learning and Skills Council for large financial deals. The LSC provides an important governance role, asking questions about the affordability, viability and value for money of projects.

Further education colleges are also governed by a board. Originally these boards were large bodies with a focus on representing stakeholder's (such as users, LEA, staff and funders) views. After incorporation in 1993 boards of governors became free of LEA involvement and were designed to have more of a business focus (Further Education Funding Council 1999). This led to accusations of a 'democratic deficit' in FE, which was accompanied by some questionable practices that became known as the 'franchising scandals' (House of Commons 1998), and some high losses incurred by colleges. The regulatory system is now moving back towards greater co-ordination and planning.

FE colleges are able to borrow by providing their assets as security on loans, although it is doubtful whether government would ever stand by and let education colleges to be sold off to the private sector if they were unable to service these loans. FE colleges are a low risk business, able to demonstrate a secure income from both LSC grants and user fees.

Education Capital Finance PLC is a funding intermediary for the further education sector. It raises finance for college development from banks and lends to colleges for capital projects. Education Capital Finance is an interesting form of Public Interest Company, a share trust. It operates as a holding company organised as a private limited company with nominal share capital held in trust. This holding company owns 100 per cent of the operating company which operates as a typical PLC. The trust is established in favour of public interest further education purposes, and independent trustees are obliged to act in accordance with these instructions. The board consists of representatives of Further Education Colleges and the Association of Colleges.

The PIC experiment in further education has largely been successful, but it has not been without its problems. For example, many good quality staff left further education to establish their own companies, selling services back to the sector (Gravatt 2002). Education Capital Finance only began lending to colleges in 2001, but business was slower than expected and its financial outlook is unclear.

3. Governance and accountability

Background

Shareholders in typical companies fulfil two vital roles; they provide risk capital and they provide corporate governance. Questions surrounding how to deal with risk in the absence of shareholders are discussed in the next chapter. This chapter examines how and whether Public Interest Companies, which do not normally have shareholders, can provide for effective corporate governance.

In theory at least, in typical companies shareholders provide directors with a clear target of increasing shareholder value, and if directors fail to deliver this increased value they can be dismissed. The absence of shareholders in most types of Public Interest Company mean that corporate governance has to be organised differently. Alternatives, such as stakeholder members without a financial interest in the organisation are considered by those opposed to Public Interest Companies as being too unfocussed and unable to take tough decisions. Yet supporters of Public Interest Companies claim that stakeholder governance, particularly if it includes direct public involvement, can increase the accountability of public services and counter the potentially harmful profit-maximising influence of shareholders.

Corporate governance in typical companies

In a company limited by shares the shareholders own the company and appoint directors to run the company on their behalf. Directors in turn appoint managers to organise the day-to-day activities of the company. Corporate governance is supposed to provide the necessary checks and balances between these groups. At an Annual General Meeting, shareholders re-appoint the board, vote on the report and accounts presented by the board, appoint auditors, and vote on any other matters that are put to them (Warren 2000). Another critical element of corporate governance is the use of independent non-executive directors, who share joint responsibility with executive directors but who are not involved in the active running of the company. They are designed to hold executive directors to account within the boardroom.

If a company is a *private* limited company, rather than a *public* limited company, it means the shares are not offered for sale on an exchange but rather are held privately by a small group of people, who are often executive directors. In cases such as this there is less separation between shareholders and directors, which can have repercussions on the effectiveness of corporate governance.

The theoretical advantage of corporate governance in the PLC model is simple: there is separation between the owners and the directors of the company, and directors are absolutely clear about the requirements of the owners – to enhance returns through an increase in the value of their shares and/or though receiving dividend payments. If directors do not deliver the requirements of the shareholders, then the owners' rights to hire and fire directors are intended to put this potential problem right.

Problems of typical corporate governance

The mechanisms of corporate governance in Public Limited Companies do not always work as theory might suggest.

PLCs often have a large number of small investors, and it can be difficult for these shareholders to organise themselves to take collective action against the directors. In comparison to other European countries the UK has very dispersed share ownership (La Porta 1998). This situation is compounded by the fact that institutions such as pension funds, who own around 70 per cent of equity funds, manage many small investors' shares. Institutional investors often take little active interest in the management of the companies they own, preferring instead to concentrate on buying and selling shares according to price signals. As a result, it is not unheard of for some institutional investors to not even turn up to the Annual General Meetings of PLCs.

In a recent study undertaken for the Department for Trade and Industry's Company Law Review, Julian Franks and Colin Mayer highlight the inability of shareholders to affect management change even when it is desired (Franks 2000). They point to 'insider' shareholdings by executive directors as a cause of this inertia. But they also point to the reluctance of shareholders to confront management over poor performance because of the effects of bad publicity and the difficulty of co-ordinating the other shareholders.

However, even the laissez-faire attitude of institutional shareholders does bring some accountability. Directors know that if their share price falls because of poor results then their company is more likely to be bought by new shareholders who may well sack the board on their acquisition. This gives directors an incentive to perform, although too often it can give them an incentive to keep the short-term share price of the company high in order to prevent take-overs. This can sometimes be at the expense of long-term health of the company.

In the wake of the collapse of Enron and other corporate scandals, the independence and effectiveness of non-executive directors has been questioned. Contrary to evidence from the USA, Franks and Mayer's study found 'no evidence of disciplining by non-executive directors', even when non-executive directors dominated the board. They partly attribute this to the inability of UK shareholders to sue UK directors for failing to fulfil their responsibilities. Franks and Mayer conclude that corporate governance in the UK relies more on technical assessments by banks and rating agencies when new financing is required rather than on boards, non-executive directors or large shareholders.

Such is the concern about the inability of institutional shareholders to hold management to account that commentators such as Harvard Business School's Michael Jensen has called for a return to highly leveraged companies (that is, companies with less equity and more debt). This is based on the observation that, contrary to expectations, lenders are better at monitoring and enforcing the actions of management. Jensen concludes that the separation of owners and managers can lead to expensive conflict rather than efficient scrutiny (Jensen, 1997). He also concludes that the typical Public Limited Company is unsuitable in a number of scenarios, including areas where long-term growth is slow (which is the case in most public services).

Assessments of the potential for corporate governance in PICs need to avoid the idealisation of governance in typical companies. Governance in PICs has its problems, but so too does that in regular corporate forms.

Corporate governance in Public Interest Companies

The methods of corporate governance within PICs are as varied as the types of PIC available.

A common example of how corporate governance works in PICs can be seen in Companies Limited by Guarantee. Here, appointed 'members' fulfil the same roles and duties as shareholders. Members have no financial stake in the business, and must pay out a fixed sum if the company goes bankrupt (often a notional payment of £1). Beyond this, however, there is much flexibility about how they are organised. For example, members can also be the directors on the board. PICs such as The Registry Trust, the organisation that disseminates information on county court judgements, are organised in this way. Alternatively, members are often given no authority over the direct management of the company, and their role is restricted to infrequent 'members' meetings'. Members might be chosen from the general public, or from a range of stakeholders, perhaps including staff, industry experts, the general public, users, and government.

Our discussions about corporate governance within Public Interest Companies revolve around three key issues:

- the extent to which PICs lack the presumed advantages of shareholder models

- the extent to which PICs can compensate for the failings of typical corporate governance

- the way in which PICs might lead to greater accountability through public involvement

---

Case study 3: The Registry Trust

The Registry Trust has kept county court judgements against people defaulting on payments since 1852, but it became a Company Limited by Guarantee and has operated as a Public Interest Company since 1986. The Trust sells information about people convicted of defaulting on payments to credit rating agencies who in turn help lenders assess credit ratings.

Interestingly the Registry Trust is organised along the lines of a Consumer Service Corporation (see pages 64-66), although unlike most it is not a utility. Users of the service, including credit reference companies and lenders, appoint the members who are also the directors. A non-executive chairman is charged with representing the public interest

---

Facing up to the problems of PIC governance

The potential problems of corporate governance in PICs stem from the fact that the owners of a PIC – the members – will have no significant financial interest in the business. Indeed, in the case of Companies Limited by Guarantee, members are forbidden from benefiting financially.

In contrast, one of the great benefits of the shareholder model is that profit is a single unifying objective of all the owners of the business. Management is always clear what the owners want from the business.

The lack of financial incentives can pose particular problems when the voluntary principle is extended from not just governance but into the boardroom. The Housing Corporation is currently consulting on whether Housing Associations, where boards are unpaid, should be able to recompense directors (Housing Corporation 2002).

In Public Interest Companies there is unlikely to be a single overriding objective shared amongst members, particularly if members consist of a range of stakeholders taken from outside the organisation. Whilst in some industries (such as air traffic control) all the stakeholders may share similar aims, in some industries (such as rail) hostile industrial relations and ideological issues may ensure that stakeholders rarely share a common view.

Opponents of PICs have pejoratively termed these stakeholder memberships 'rainbow coalitions', with some justification. Stakeholder governance can be a headache for managers if they receive conflicting signals about priorities, and also for lenders who can be suspicious of the ability of the board to take the tough financial decisions necessary to safeguard their funds.

Because their own resources are not at risk, there may be a tendency for members to put off difficult decisions and to succumb to boardroom inertia. Renewal of the board and management is an important aspect of private companies, yet in PICs there can be a tendency for members to become defenders of the status quo rather than agents for change. These problems can be compounded if members also have a place on the board.

Neither are opponents of PICs short of examples of where stakeholder governance has failed to deliver results. David Leam at the Social Market Foundation highlights how unwieldy stakeholder boards, paralysed by disagreements and unable to take difficult decisions, exacerbated the problems in the California energy crisis of 2001 (Leam 2002).

Attractions of PIC governance

Despite these concerns, there are a number of areas where the governance arrangements in Public Interest Companies might offer advantages over traditional corporate governance.

It is sometimes doubted whether directors and management can be properly incentivised in Public Interest Companies. In companies limited by shares, key staff will often receive part of their salaries as shares of the company. That way they have a personal incentive to improve the value of the company, which aligns their interests with those of the company's owners. The absence of shares makes this approach impossible in Companies Limited by Guarantee, potentially weakening the corporate governance arrangements. Nonetheless, it is not difficult to continue to provide incentive bonuses when certain desirable financial conditions are met. For example in Glas Cymru, the Welsh water utility and PIC, directors are rewarded financially if there is a growth in financial reserves (Glas Cymru 2001).

A positive feature of PIC governance is that management rewards do not have to be restricted to such financial considerations. In Glas Cymru again, half of a director's bonuses are dependent on how well the company delivers services to customers, measured by the overall service performance assessed and published by the water regulator, OFWAT (Glas Cymru 2001). Using management bonuses in this way can mean public service quality can be incentivised directly, rather than being a presumed correlate of a high share price. In monopoly utilities the lack of competition can result in a significant divergence between shareholders interest and the public interest, so particularly in these environments a mixture of financial and public service performance criteria can make management more effective than might otherwise be the case.

Members of a PIC that have a particular self-interest in the success of the organisation can take a more active interest in governance arrangements than might regular shareholders. Examples of self-interest might include organisations where staff are given a role in governing the organisation, either on their own as an employee co-operative, or alongside other stakeholders. Staff, particularly in the public sector, may have an interest in the wider aims of the organisation and be able to highlight inefficiencies because of their insider knowledge. Allowing staff to become 'co-producers' may also improve motivation. However, there are substantial problems with giving staff a large say in the governance of an organisation. They can be resistant to change, particularly where tough management decisions are required, and there is a danger of producer capture, where staff run the organisation more in their own interests than in the interests of the consumer.

Another type of self-interest that can make Public Interest Company members better corporate governors than profit-seeking shareholders is where the member is a corporate user of a service and has a significant financial interest in ensuring the business performs well and performs efficiently. This type of arrangement can be seen in the Consumer Service Corporations discussed on pages 64-66, which are particularly suitable for monopoly utilities.

Lenders and corporate governance

In the absence of shareholders who normally carry out governance duties in typical companies, lenders – who likewise might have significant sums invested in PICs – might be expected to fulfil an effective governance role.

Lenders take little interest in corporate governance in typical companies as their money is likely to be repaid regardless of the day-to-day fortunes of the company. As discussed in Chapter 4 on finance and risk in PICs, lenders are unlikely to bear any more risk in PICs than they do in typical companies. Therefore, if lenders are given a role in a Public Interest Company's corporate governance it should be done with extreme caution.

Lenders might be the only group with any financial stake in a PIC, and they may play a useful role in financial scrutiny, especially during the process of deciding whether or not to invest. After this point, however, they should not be relied upon to fulfil the same duties with the same attention to detail as shareholders.

Case study 4: Housing Associations

Housing associations are one of the oldest types of Public Interest Company, with associations such as the Peabody Housing Trust established in 1862, and the Guinness Trust established in 1890. In the last twenty years there has been a large shift from the public provision of social housing to provision by housing associations. Housing associations in 2002 accounted for 1.5 million homes, around 7 per cent of the housing stock in England, compared to just 2 per cent in 1981 (Duckworth 2002).

The Government's preference for housing associations over local authority delivered social housing over this period was essentially for two reasons: to get social housing investment off the Government's balance sheet, and to avoid what was seen as poor housing management by local authorities.

A decision by the Treasury in 1986 to allow housing associations to borrow using private finance without this appearing on the Government's balance sheet was a defining moment. Previously, investment by housing associations had been restrained by government borrowing restrictions. The Conservative Government's subsequent Social Housing Act of 1988 permitted a mixed approach to financing housing associations. In the subsequent years this has resulted in £23 billion of private finance, a large amount similar to all private investment in the PFI by 2002.

Housing associations are widely regarded as a successful development in the social housing sector. They provide a useful example of a widely used form of Public Interest Company and they provide some lessons for the use of this model in other public service areas.

Effects of the 1988 changes

The introduction of private finance and other changes to housing associations in 1988 had a rapid and significant impact on the size, shape and activities of the sector. Not only did the provision of housing by housing associations expand, but the nature of housing association management changed as directors were free to set their own priorities (Mullins 2000).

New housing projects were no longer solely funded centrally through the Housing Corporation's Approved Development Plans. Instead, new projects were financed through private investment, funded largely from rental income (heavily subsidised through government housing benefit payments) and local authority grants. This gave associations a freedom to shop around to make their investments as productive as possible. Partly as a result of these pressures housing associations, which previously had tended to be located in specific areas, became much more geographically dispersed. Even the newer large scale voluntary stock transfer (LSVT) associations that used to be owned by individual councils have diversified into new geographical areas.

The 1988 changes also meant that associations could pursue other non-housing income streams. Many associations (for some time) have offered other services to tenants, such as training and employment advice. However, some housing associations are now becoming much more diverse in the services they offer. The Places for People group, for instance, now delivers not just social housing, but also market rented housing and housing for sale. This helps cross-subsidise more affordable housing and helps provide mixed tenure estates. It also delivers other services such as nurseries. Many associations are taking advantage of their 'not-for-profit' status, stakeholder governance and strong balance sheets to become key partners in government regeneration programmes, such as the New Deal for Communities, which can bring in significant new income streams. Such is the extent and potential of these new services that many associations have now dropped the word 'housing' from their names.

The use of private finance has also led to internal changes in associations. Banks have required more detailed business plans and evidence of sound financial planning before being willing to invest in projects. Associations have been keen to reduce costs through stock rationalisation, achieving economies of scale and through other avenues.

Associations are also now much more complex organisations. Three-quarters of all housing association homes are now part of a formal grouping of two or more organisations. For example, some associations have a number of subsidiary companies, whilst others have entered into partnerships with other associations (Audit Commission 2001). In part this has been to escape charitable status restrictions on trading, but a key driver behind the process has been the need to either spread or ring-fence risk. For example, the use of subsidiary companies for new non-social housing ventures can help prevent risks being borne by the core business. Meanwhile, group structures that bring together a number of smaller associations result in wider asset bases and can help pool risk and result in cheaper borrowing.

Private finance and risk

Whilst the introduction of private finance has clearly had an impact on housing associations, it would be wrong to over emphasise any transfer of risk onto private lenders. In order to get housing association investment off balance sheet government had to provide adequate risk transfer from the Government to the associations, alongside proven operational independence. However, as suggested on page 58, lenders are reluctant to bear these risks, and this has clearly been the case in the housing association sector. Indeed, in over a decade no lender has lost money in the sector.

Risks have instead been dealt with in a variety of ways, as discussed below. In particular, some significant risks have been transferred to tenants, who have seen their rents increase:

● The old regime whereby local authority officers set housing association rents was changed so that the associations themselves could vary rent levels. Because housing association rents were significantly below market rent levels this transferred risk to the associations (more accurately the tenants) and away from the Government. It also provided a useful financial buffer which could be accessed in times of need, or which could be used to accumulate surpluses. This policy has now been reversed and rent increases are restricted for all associations.

● The old housing associations had very healthy balance sheets with significant reserves accumulated over a century which could be relied upon in difficult times.

● The Government's Social Housing Grant is formulated as a subordinated loan to housing associations. As a result lenders are confident that they will receive their payments before government if an association got into difficulty. In effect, this is a substantial government guarantee, even though the value of the grant has declined in recent years.

- Government housing benefit payments covering the rent of low income tenants also act as government support. This level of support is significant as over two-thirds of housing association tenants receive housing benefit.
- The Housing Corporation has significant regulatory powers and helps ensure associations do not get into financial difficulty. For those that do, the Corporation helps resolve the situation without catastrophic failure.
- Housing stock acts as collateral. In theory at least, if an association gets into financial difficulty homes could be sold off to ensure lenders received their payments. Intervention from the Housing Corporation has meant that no tenant has lost their home in recent times. Although it is never made explicit, this brings with it a presumption on behalf of the private sector that social housing has a government guarantee. Banks presume that it would be difficult for any government to sit by and allow social housing tenants to be thrown out of their homes and their buildings sold off because of financial mismanagement.

Despite the degree of security for private lenders, unfamiliarity with the sector meant that lenders were slow to take up the offer of providing finance. New organisations such as the Housing Finance Corporation (itself a form of PIC) were established to facilitate the new market. Although the number of lenders involved in this market is small, there are now highly specialised teams who are eager to lend.

The position of the newer large scale voluntary stock transfer (LSVT) associations is different from the older associations. Tenants are required to vote in favour of stock transfer, and they receive guarantees on rents remaining at local authority levels for a set period of time. In addition, unlike the older associations they are not blessed with healthy balance sheets. This significantly alters the risk profiles of these organisations, and they might be more vulnerable than the older associations.

The new mixed financing arrangements have, in their own terms, been successful; a large amount of private finance has been provided at decent rates, and the level of the social housing grant has fallen (Whitehead 1999).

Results
It is difficult to make claims about the relative success or otherwise of the management of housing associations. Whilst they have offered an alternative to council housing departments, their comparative performance has been mixed. Housing associations perform better than local authority owned housing in terms of tenant satisfaction, but the difference is modest.[4]

Importantly, managers of housing associations have significant freedoms over how they structure their organisation, whether they should diversify into new geographical areas or into the provision of new types of services. Compared to local authority owned housing, there is also more clarity over the roles and responsibilities of housing managers.

However, there have been criticisms that associations are less accountable to their tenants than local authority owned housing, although the type and extent of accountability structures and outcomes varies hugely. In some areas the plethora of housing associations has made developing strategic regeneration plans more difficult than it might have been if social housing was solely provided by councils, although this may be an acceptable trade-off if performance in those local areas has improved (Murie 2002).

Tenants have seen rising rent levels, but have benefited from investment which might not have been made available under the previous borrowing regime. Another factor has been that the large range of types of housing association have provided a good deal of diversity in the sector. The Housing Corporation has played a key role in providing comparisons between providers, and has facilitated a degree of contestability, encouraging mergers and acquisitions where associations have failed to provide an adequate service.

The future

The history of housing associations is interesting in relation to the current debates about the use of Public Interest Companies in other fields. However, the housing association sector is still developing and its future poses some difficult issues, particularly in relation to diversification and accountability.

It is unclear where the eagerness of some housing associations to diversify into new service delivery areas will lead. The Housing Corporation has indicated that it expects housing associations to keep the provision of social housing as their primary activity, and that associations should not diversify to the extent that activities other than social housing become a rival or dominant activity (Housing Corporation 1999). Meanwhile the Government has encouraged associations to become actively involved in regeneration projects and to access other sources of funding, and many associations have shown themselves well placed to deliver these services.

But how far might diversification go? Might housing associations one day seek to deliver other types of public service, such as clinical care or mainstream education? Whilst this is possible, it may not be advisable. The history of public service organisations (or indeed private firms) diversifying into other areas is not good. Privatised utilities like the water companies were eager to diversify as their core operations were essentially low yield businesses and these activities were also constrained by regulators. However, most of these developments did not meet with success, and, as described elsewhere in this report in the case study on Glas Cymru, lenders have factored in the costs of failed diversification into the costs of finance. Regeneration activities, providing housing for 'key-workers', and community education and training carried out by housing associations are either reliant on, or close to, the core skills of associations. However, providing more ambitious services might prove a step too far. The Housing Corporation as regulator is right to advise caution in these matters.

Meanwhile, other recent developments provide the prospect of even greater diversity in the social housing sector. Local authorities are now able to form local authority housing companies, known as Arms-Length Management Organisations (ALMOs) which create a separation between the commissioning and provision of council housing, but councils retain a degree of control. Besides council representatives on the board, others such as tenants, representatives of the local community, independents, and local businesses are also represented. These companies can combine strategic local authority control to develop better synergy with local regeneration strategies with tenant involvement and still have the financial flexibility for investment to appear off the Government's balance sheet (ODPM 2003).

A second interesting future development concerns participation and accountability. The older housing associations were designed as rather paternalistic organisations, and have minimal tenant participation on boards. Any members are usually co-opted rather than directly elected. In newer stock transfer associations, however, a third of the board represents tenants, usually as a result of a direct vote. This greater user participation is partly designed to make tenant ballots on the question of stock transfer more palatable to tenants, but they are also used to improve governance and counter criticisms that housing associations are less accountable than typical council housing.

Tenant involvement in social housing governance is a mixed picture; for every dynamic group of tenants keeping housing management on their toes, there are some sorry meetings attended by a few unrepresentative activists who do little to communicate the needs of tenants. Some of the older housing associations have acknowledged their need to make services more responsive to tenants, but have taken action through other routes besides direct tenant governance. For example the Peabody Housing Trust has used devices such as tenant satisfaction surveys and focus groups to provide more responsive services. New tenant participation compacts provide a formal definition between the rights and responsibilities of both associations and their tenants.

It could be argued that the key to making social housing more responsive and accountable to tenants is not through either governance or surveys, but is by providing social housing tenants with greater choices over their housing provider. There are currently moves to allow tenants to choose their social housing provider, although this is only likely to provide a real solution in parts of the north of England and the midlands where there is excess capacity.

Conclusion

As a result of changes made to the sector over the last two decades, housing associations now deliver over a third of all social housing in England. Whilst the performance of the sector is mixed, associations have proved themselves able to respond to a new environment. They have unleashed a good deal of entrepreneurial activity, particularly with regard to accessing new income streams.

The sector provides a number of useful lessons for the use of Public Interest Companies in other public service areas:

- Providing the sector with financial and managerial freedoms has led to a burst of innovation and unexpected activity. Whilst these new freedoms have not resulted in clear success for all associations, the sector is performing well and is confident of its future. Managers in other areas of the public services are likely to look upon the freedoms enjoyed by housing association managers with envy.
- The use of private finance has clearly led to some changes to managerial decisions. The insistence of high quality risk and business analysis has helped the sector improve its focus in these areas. Whilst lenders bear little risk in the activities of the older housing associations in particular, they have provided some incentives to improve efficiency and understand risk.

- Whilst associations are likely to continue to diversify into other service delivery activity, this diversification may prove problematic if associations stray too far from their core activity and knowledge. Whilst there should be nothing to fear intrinsically from associations becoming more heavily involved in delivering key services such as health, social services or education, the Government and its regulators should keep a close eye on the quality of services delivered. Caution in this area is well placed. Whilst the Housing Corporation's current position in preventing other service activity from becoming the main activity of associations may prove too prescriptive, government should ensure that the delivery of key taxpayer-funded public services by all PICs, including housing associations, are covered by similar independent regulators.
- Housing associations have proved adept at developing new income streams from private provision. Whilst this may be appropriate in housing, it may prove problematic in other areas; for example, an expansion in privately funded healthcare might undermine support for the NHS. Government will want to pay attention to the development of any unregulated private activity in other types of PIC.
- Geographical diversification and the invention of complex group structures have proved to be important parts of the new freedoms available to housing associations. However, these have led to some accountability problems (Audit Commission 2001). The future of a public service market where PICs are used may end up looking very different to how government and others initially expect. Accountability mechanisms must be capable of withstanding such pressures.
- It remains in doubt whether tenants and the wider public understand the hybrid position associations occupy between the public and private sectors. For example when groups such as Defend Council Housing oppose large-scale voluntary stock transfer they paint the process as 'privatisation', even though there are clearly significant differences between housing associations and shareholder-owned profit-maximising companies. The success of these 'anti-privatisation' campaigns demonstrates how fragile the legitimacy of the Public Interest Company structure can be. It is not only important that PICs are accountable, well-governed organisations; they need to be seen to be such if they are to fulfil their public interest role.

Whilst in some areas the experience of housing associations is instructive, the lessons of housing associations should not be over emphasised. Crucially, housing associations are unusual in having a funding stream reliant on private individuals who are to the large part subsidised by government. This makes them different from other PICs solely reliant on taxpayer funding. Taxpayer-funded PICs are (rightly) unlikely to be judged as off the Government's balance sheet, so private financing is unlikely to offer the same advantages (see p70) or opportunities.

However, the degree to which the freedoms and activities of the housing associations are dependent on private finance is anyway debatable. It is arguable that it is the encouragement of markets and of managerial freedoms that have that has led to this new dynamism in the sector. If adequate finance was provided directly by government through appropriate mechanisms, then similar benefits might occur. This, though, is a highly unlikely circumstance, as confirmed by the Deputy Prime Minister's announcement that local authorities will not be able to use new prudential borrowing frameworks to benefit council housing (ODPM 2003; *Public Finance* 2003).

Public involvement

Potential benefits

Perhaps the most significant justification for the alternative governance arrangements possible in a Public Interest Company is the potential role that public users of a service, or the wider community, can play.

Some members of the public have a passionate interest in the success of public organisations even though they have no financial stake. Lincoln City FC is now organised as a mutual football club, with fans owning and controlling the organisation. There are also 60 football trusts set up by fans, 32 of which have shareholdings in their clubs and 22 of which are represented on the board of the club. Although they do not deliver a public service, these professional football clubs are an example where public control could be highly effective (Football Governance Research Centre 2002). Football fans are passionately interested in the success of their club, they will follow their team through good times and bad, and are often able to suffer short term pain if they know it is in the long-term interests of the club.

It is more difficult to find examples of public services where users are quite so passionate, or would be willing to prioritise the long term over the short term. One example, however, might be the 60 'public interest' members of Network Rail. These appointed members have to demonstrate a strong interest in the rail network and its management. Not simply representatives of user groups, these public members could be expected to give greater scrutiny over management decisions than institutional investors in Railtrack ever did.

There are those that argue that such involvement of the public in the governance of public services represents a radical new way of ensuring accountability and open government. Some have even proposed that the great majority of public services could be organised in this way (Mayo 2001).

There are certainly advantages in making public services more open. Secrecy or opaqueness in public services can too often disguise waste and poor quality. Enabling a direct flow of information from the management of the service to the public or service users is a way to keep public managers alert to their responsibilities.

Giving service users a direct role in governance is also an effective way to ensure that users views about the service are really taken into account by management. State institutions too often presume they are operating in the interests of users by virtue of the fact that they are publicly owned. Being forced to listen to the views of users is potentially very helpful. Likewise, private contractors delivering contracts to local or central government can be guided by the contract alone, and neglect communication direct with users. Again, the PICs can be an effective way of bringing stakeholders into the decision making process.

Stakeholder involvement is not just about trying to improve the technical quality of services, or to attempt to make services more responsive to the needs of users. It is also inextricably linked to notions of trust. Henry Hansmann's seminal US study highlighted the important role that nonprofits (his term roughly equates to our charitable sector) play in retaining public trust in institutions where, because of informational asymmetries of other reasons, users would not be able to judge quality for themselves in a private sector environment. Such concerns about the quality of public services are similar to those represented earlier in Chapter 2, which discusses the potential problems of incomplete contracts.

Hansmann also evokes a wider spirit of public trust in public service institutions, a point analysed in more detail in a recent paper prepared for the Prime Minister's Strategy Unit on the concept of Public Value. The Strategy Unit paper highlights the importance that people feel 'connected' with the public services and that they feel trustful of the public realm, regardless of what type of institution delivers the service (Kelly 2002). Ministers have made much of the argument that PICs can increase public feelings of ownership and connection to public services in their justifications of the new NHS foundation trusts (Milburn 2002b). If PICs did not result in a statistical improvement in the quality of a public service, but were able to improve feelings of trust and ownership over public services then they might still be considered a success.

Unfortunately, there is no convincing empirical evidence to suggest that PICs are more loved than other types of organisation. Indeed, housing associations, which are some of the oldest types of PIC, are not widely understood to be 'not-for-profit' organisations. In tenant ballots on large scale voluntary stock transfer, opposition movements have successfully portrayed transfer as privatisation and defeated transfer proposals. In addition, BUPA, the private health care operator is a mutual organisation which now delivers some limited public services under contract to the NHS. It is doubtful whether BUPA receives a more favourable public image on account of its PIC status.

Despite the lack of evidence, by promoting direct links between users of a service and the governance of the institution we might expect well run PICs to engender a greater sense of legitimacy to some types of public service. Although again far from proven, they might also be expected to give greater protection of the elusive principle of the 'public service ethos' than in typical private sector companies.

High levels of trust between the public and existing charitable organisations can be utilised by the public sector through PICs. For example, with the help of the Improvement and Development Agency (IDeA), IPPR and the New Economics Foundation, the London Borough of Tower Hamlets is putting in place a new procurement regime designed to increase the amount of service delivery by carried out by charities and other community organisations. The council aims to use these existing organisations to reach out to the many deprived and diverse communities in the council that presently do not have good access to council services. The council presumes that communities do not access these services either because they do not trust the council, or they do not know such services exist. Delivering services using these other trusted groups could help improve take up. It might also allow a better two-way communication between users and the council as to what types of services are required.

For many PICs, particularly smaller-scale regeneration organisations, the primary aim of the organisation will be to increase trust and social capital in order to provide deprived communities with better skills and increased social cohesion. The corporate efficiency of such organisations is arguably a lower priority. The stakeholder membership possible in PICs is an ideal way to structure such companies. More difficult issues surrounding the quality of governance or matters of finance are much less of an issue to these smaller organisations.

Potential difficulties of public involvement in PIC governance

One potential source of difficulty with stakeholder governance is that discussions often confuse corporate governance with involvement in day-to-day management. Proper corporate governance might only consist of arms-length involvement; for example shareholders who provide corporate governance in typical companies usually meet only annually to appoint the board and auditors and to comment on major strategic decisions. Public accountability and trust might actually be worsened if PICs are promoted as interactive organisations, yet the public is only required to attend one meeting a year and comment on auditing matters.

There is also a key issue about who is chosen to be a public member, and whether they are suitable and representative. The few PIC-like institutions in existence already struggle to attract public members. The Housing Corporation is having to consider providing remuneration for board members. Where volunteers can be found, they are often the 'great and the good'; the same faces involved representing public views in schools, housing associations and charities. This raises an important point about the representativeness of any public members. The 'great and the good' are typically middle class, self-selecting and able to subsidise any voluntary work from higher incomes. Priorities may well differ between classes, say between providing user choice or providing a high quality of service to the very poorest. It might also lead to good governance in wealthy areas, and poor governance in the poorer areas; indeed IPPR's recent publication on school governance concluded that governing bodies were least effective where they were most needed (Hallgarten 2000).

Although a public service crisis or major event such as the building of a new facility can drum up community interest and help provide a good range of people in the initial period, there are questions as to whether this level of interest can be sustained in the long term. The continual involvement of a parent with a child's school might help promote long-term interest, but the infrequent relationship that most of the community has with a local hospital is less likely to engender an enthusiastic response over a long period of time; particularly if the hospital is managed well and not subject to critical local media attention. Whilst the interest of the general public in helping maintain the quality of their local institutions should not be underestimated, there is a real doubt there is a sufficient pool of eager and suitable members of the public to provide capacity for a large expansion in Public Interest Companies.

Even if there were a group of people willing to become PIC members, with turnout for local elections hovering around 30 per cent there is considerable doubt as to whether the general public has any appetite to elect them, or even complain if they fail to carry out their duties effectively.

More dangerously, without the same level of legal scrutiny that public elections receive, there is arguably a raised possibility of fraud and corruption if these public members control important public services. Despite the many criticisms levelled at them, both central and local government are legitimate and publicly accountable. Corruption is rare and severely punished. The same might not be the case for loosely scrutinised PICs.

Good corporate governance depends on governors understanding their business and being prepared to ask tough questions of management. The failure of this process in typical for-profit companies has led to much recent media attention and a government inquiry (Higgs 2003). However, there is a thin line between effective scrutiny and dangerous hostility in corporate governance. If PIC members are elected, and especially if turnout is low or there are few candidates, there is a potential problem that members will not act in the general public interest but will represent pressure groups with a distinct agenda. If such activists oppose the basic premise of the PIC then the organisation could get into severe difficulty.

Anticipating this problem in the passionate debate about the future of the railways, Network Rail's independent public members have to be broadly acceptable to the board. As a result a strange circular accountability ensues where the members appoint the board, but the board can veto members. This curious situation has been criticised by the New Economics Foundation as 'worse than Enron' (New Economics Foundation 2002). This is far from the case – the governance structures of Network Rail are a significant improvement in those of Railtrack – but thought needs to be given as to how such a situation can be avoided. Approving members in accordance with the 'Nolan principles' of standards in public life could provide a way in which the quality, independence and integrity of public members could help be ensured in a PIC (see Committee on Standards in Public Life, www.public-standards.gov.uk for details).

There are less insidious ways in which special interest groups can capture public governors. For example, the traditionally paternalistic relationship between hospital consultants and patients could result in the public members and governors of an NHS foundation trusts becoming the 'doctor's champions' instead of representing the views of the wider community and holding consultants and hospital managers to account. When dealing with such emotive matters it will be a brave public member who challenges consultants that want extra investment in particular services, even though the major advantage might be to those consultants' reputation rather than the local community's health needs.

It is also important that thought is put into which aspect of a public service receives stakeholder inclusion. Again, in the debate over NHS foundation trusts arguably too much attention has been placed onto giving the acute sector public legitimacy, whilst the commissioning end, the Primary Care Trusts, who purchase services on behalf of citizens have been a secondary thought. Giving greater strength to the acute sector is potentially unwise when many health experts consider that more resources should be invested in preventative care rather than acute care. Arguments about changing resource priorities may become even more difficult if stakeholder members become the public champions of hospital interests.

Separation of accountability and governance

Promoters of Public Interest Companies often assume that by including the public in the governance of an organisation that organisation will be more accountable and responsive to users. As discussed above, there are pros and cons to this approach. However, too often in discussions the questions of accountability and governance are conflated, yet they remain separate issues.

In *Building Better Partnerships* IPPR identified three types of accountability in relation to public private partnerships:

- Transparency: organisations that deliver public services are required to disclose key information, making their decisions open to public scrutiny

- Responsibility: there should be clarity as to the organisation or individual that is answerable for particular decisions and courses of action.

- Responsiveness: services are able to adapt to reflect citizens' needs, priorities, and expectations.

Stakeholder governance is often regarded as a good way to deliver more responsive services. As set out above there are clear instances where this is both possible and even probable. However, there are other ways to make services more responsive besides more inclusive governance, even when delivered by PICs.

For instance, there are sophisticated methods of giving service users and other stakeholders a channel of communication into the heart of a company, without the necessity of becoming a PIC and bringing the complex problems that come through an absence of shareholders. The Social Market Foundation has highlighted how two-tier stakeholder boards offer such a possibility (Leam 2002). Such organisations might provide a policy solution where stakeholder inclusion is desired but where PICs are not suitable for other reasons.

Some have also cast doubt on whether any kind of formal stakeholder governance is required in order to make services highly responsive and accountable. For example, tenant meetings in housing associations have a mixed reputation and are frequently poorly attended, which can affect their representativeness. Yet tenant responsiveness and satisfaction can be monitored through other means such as user satisfaction surveys, focus groups and more direct interaction.

In some ways it is a strange response to assume that the poorest in our society have a great desire to attend meetings to help decide public service management priorities. We do not assume that other sections of society have a similar desire, even when they might have more skills and time available to make an impact on the quality of those services. Higher income groups assume that if a particular service provider is not delivering they will be able to find another higher quality provider. User choice and contestability (being able to replace a poorly performing service provider) may in the end be a greater spur for accountability than stakeholder governance alone.

PICs and democratic accountability

The role of (local) government

If the use of Public Interest Companies becomes widespread there is a possibility that a complex mass of public governance organisations will come into being, many of which will operate at a local level.

Some in local government are concerned about such a possibility.

Having only recently been told that they should be focussed on the strategic overview of services, rather than their public provision, local authorities might be reluctant to share this strategic role with a range of alternative institutions, including service users, industry representatives and financiers.

Moreover, PIC public governance bodies will be attached to their individual services, and it is unlikely that work between services will be co-ordinated. The proliferation of public trusts and bodies was one of the reasons why local authorities were developed in the Victorian era. Local government representatives, including Sir Jeremy Beecham, the Chairman of the Local Government Association, have warned that PICs will lead to a further erosion of their powers and influence in addition to making it more difficult to co-ordinate fractured public services in their community (*Financial Times* 2003).

In some ways, local authorities are right to be wary. Reducing what was at the time seen as the malign influence of local government was a key driver behind the expansion of PICs such as housing associations and further education colleges in the 1980s and early 1990s. However, it is not just local government in the firing line; one of the arguments behind new NHS foundation trusts is to reduce central government's influence as well.

There is clearly a tension between co-ordinating public interest bodies and providing them with the freedom to operate outside local (or central) bureaucracies. Whilst some co-ordination by local government may become desirable if the use of PICs proliferates, the desire to use new types of governance offers a lesson for government at all levels. Government needs to modernise and prove that it can adequately represent the interests of the local community, and not just serve its own bureaucratic needs. If government opened itself up to greater public involvement and scrutiny there might be less desire for these alternative forms of governance.

Both central and local government will and should, however, continue to play a vital role in PIC governance. This can be seen in the local authority role within new local housing companies (ALMOs) and government influence via the Strategic Rail Authority in Network Rail. Local government should also be brought into the governance arrangements for PICs such as NHS foundation trusts. The Government, though, needs to appreciate that it does not hold a monopoly on the public interest, and other stakeholders – including the public themselves – should be seen as legitimate governance partners. PICs should not be used as a mechanism to 'escape' or 'curtail' local government, but they could help provide more diverse types of governance and ownership.

PICs and electoral accountability

Public Interest Companies, as with other types of public private partnership, can present apparent problems in that the public is unable to 'vote out' service operators that they are unhappy with. This can happen where PICs provide services under long-term contracts to a public authority (as the NHS foundation trusts will) or where they deliver services independently from government (as with housing associations).

The degree to which electoral accountability in the traditional sense ever really takes place is questionable. It is a blunt tool; the public will consider a wide range of factors when casting their vote, not just the performance of one particular public service.

IPPR has previously argued that in certain circumstances PPPs might actually increase local accountability and legitimacy (IPPR 2001). For example, the public might be given a say over the level of annual payment to contractors based on customer satisfaction levels. They might also been given a voice in deciding whether a poorly performing contractor should be replaced.

These issues could be similarly applied to PICs as well as to more typical public private partnerships, particularly where a service is being delivered under contract. Also, most PICs provide a further avenue for direct public accountability through giving users and other stakeholders a direct voice in any stakeholder governing body.

The crucial issue is that accountability to the public and to service users should be an important consideration in the development of any public service, whether provided by a public authority, a private provider, or a hybrid Public Interest Company.

Conclusion

User participation can be a useful tool in improving public services. In some instances, particularly where direct participation in governance is a key policy aim, Public Interest Companies can provide a suitable vehicle for providing this inclusion. However, stakeholder governance comes with its problems, and may not even be the most effective route to more responsive services.

The strong political movement behind the mutual and co-operative movements can make a hard-headed evaluation of the costs and benefits of stakeholder governance more difficult than it might other wise be, especially for those on the centre-left. However, many of the practical problems associated with stakeholder governance can be overcome if an organisation is designed with intelligence and foresight. Listening directly to the needs of service users is too rare in public services, regardless of what type of organisation delivers them. PICs can help put the public back into public services.

Unfortunately, public involvement in PIC governance, whilst attractive, is not simple or without its difficulties. As such, it is problematic to start justifying PICs solely on the basis of improved accountability. PICs should also demonstrate some practical policy advantage before they should be considered for any public service.

4. Finance and risk

Introduction

Questions of finance and risk are central to any understanding of the potential role of Public Interest Companies. The absence of shareholders who bear risk in typical companies have led to accusations that Public Interest Companies are an unsuitable organisational form where external finance is important. However, supporters of PICs have sited the presumed ability of PICs to escape public sector borrowing restrictions and borrow freely on the financial markets, and their supposed lower costs of finance. However, these issues are complex.

Finance is such a crucial issue because organisations, whether they are private companies or public institutions, need to invest in new infrastructure or other assets from time to time. In some cases the organisation will not have enough income in their accounts to make this investment up front. They will seek to borrow funds in the belief that increased revenue resulting from the investment will enable it to service the borrowing.

It is useful to note the difference between *funding* and *financing* in this debate as the two are often confused. The easiest way to illustrate this difference is to use a private sector example. In purchasing a car many people will use private *finance*, that is, they will borrow from a financing company the sum necessary to drive the car away. However, they will have to find the *funding* for this purchase from their own income, probably paying monthly instalments back to the financing company. That institution does not in the end provide a single penny of actual resource.

Questions of finance are inextricably linked to questions of risk. Good management aims to be able to recognise risk and have the ability to deal with it. A company's capital structure, its balance of equity and debt, is a central tool in the mitigation of risk (Gibson-Smith 2002).

The following section frequently makes assumptions that access to private sector finance markets is practical, legal and desirable. For reasons set out on page 73 this may not be desirable, particularly for taxpayer-funded PICs. It is also possible that some PICs will not require such sums for investment, for example if they have a procurement role, or if they are involving in managing non-capital intensive industries. The following part of this chapter also presumes a Public Interest Company of a certain size; these comments may not be appropriate for smaller, community-based Public Interest Companies that do not have a secure or substantial income stream.

Basics of financing in typical private sector companies

Most large private sector corporations are financed by a mixture of equity (shares) and debt (borrowing, either bonds or bank lending). Equity is risk-bearing capital; it will provide returns to shareholders in the form of dividend payments, and if a company is successful the price of these shares is likely to increase and shareholders can sell these shares on at a profit. If a company is not successful the equity acts as a buffer zone for the organisation. Dividend payments can be withheld and the share price can fall. If a company goes bust shareholders are last in line to receive any debts owed, but they retain the residual value of the company after all the other claims have been made. Equity is a risky investment; it offers the possibility of large financial rewards, but also of losses.

The providers of the risk capital will have extensive rights of ownership and control over the venture, conveyed to them by virtue of being shareholders. These rights are well understood and are generally viewed as essential to shareholders being the 'front line' bearer of risk of the activity. These rights of ownership do not mean that shareholders manage the organisation on a day to day basis, but shareholders do have the power to appoint or sack board members, appoint auditors, vote on the remuneration of directors and are consulted on the company's strategy.

Equity is an expensive form of capital as investors will expect higher returns in exchange for bearing the risks of the organisation. Although we commonly refer to risk capital as 'equity' or 'shares', there are many other types of risk capital. For example 'subordinated debt', where in cases of bankruptcy lenders only receive their payment after typical (senior) debt is paid off.

Debt is a much less risky form of borrowing for the lender. It is usually provided by banks or by a bond issue for larger companies (bonds provide a fixed annual return on investment and the return of the original sum invested – the 'principal' – at a pre-specified date). In the normal run of events debt investors have no rights of ownership over the company, and do not seek any; although they do insist on some security, such as step-in rights to take control of the company in case of severe financial difficulties. They receive their annual payments year in year out, regardless of how the company is performing. If a company goes bust, debt investors will be amongst the first in line to receive their debts from the company. As a result of the lower risks borne by debt, it is a much less costly form of borrowing.

The proportion of debt to equity borrowing is known as gearing, with 'high' gearing being a high proportion of debt to equity. The managing of share offerings, debt issues, gearing ratios and other aspects of finance is a vital and complex job in large companies.

Equity is also important in PLCs because directors are seen as best incentivised with the search for operating efficiencies if they can be sacked if they do not achieve these efficiencies and if their remuneration reflects their success in optimising performance. Debt does provide incentives, but these are less sharp. Debt investors want their money back, but they are not incentivised to extract the last pound of efficiency. In fact debt investors may not be happy about company initiatives that could be seen as too risky.

Financing in Public Interest Companies

A common feature of Public Interest Companies is that they are not supported by risk capital (or 'equity') sourced from the private sector. This means these organisations will have unusual methods of financing which are not as well understood as those used in typical private sector companies.

Larger Public Interest Companies may rely on debt financing alone. There are serious implications resulting from this, including questions about how risk is to be provided for in the absence of risk capital, and how this will impact on the costs of capital.

Assuming that there are some risks involved in the operation of a Public Interest Company, we need to identify where these risks will be borne if there is no equity. This report identifies six principal ways in which these risks can be dealt with:

- lenders could bear the risks

- sufficient cash reserves could be built up over the short term to absorb expected future risks

- financial support from taxpayers could be obtained as a substitute for risk capital

- risks could be transferred on to the users of the service

- risks could be absorbed within the operational performance of the company

- risks could be externalised, through outsourced contracts or insurance

These six options are discussed in greater detail below.

Larger Public Interest Companies do not have to rely solely on debt financing. In our categorisation of Public Interest Companies in the earlier chapter we highlighted some Public Interest Companies, such as the Post Office, which have the Government as a sole shareholder. In these cases the Government clearly bears the risk, although the experience of organisations such as the Post Office and the Royal Mint suggests that Government is not a particularly good shareholder capable of providing clear priorities to managers (Corry 2003).

Types of risk that a Public Interest Company might face

When discussing risk in Public Interest Companies we need to be aware that risks can come from a variety of sources (PricewaterhouseCoopers Corporate Finance 2002). These include

- demand risk: where demand for a service can change over time

- investment risk: where investment decisions may or may not prove to have correctly evaluated future needs

- exogenous risk: eg, legislative or regulatory risk, outside the influence of managers which can alter employment costs, or say costs associated with environmental impacts.

- operational risks: for example most PICs will be undergoing a period of structural transformation when created, for which staff will have little personal experience.

Case study 5: NHS Foundation Trusts

In January 2002 Alan Milburn MP, the Secretary of State for Health, announced plans to allow top performing NHS trusts to become foundation trusts (Milburn 2002a; Department of Health 2002a and 2002b). All NHS trusts that gained three star status from the Commission for Health Improvement (that is, the best 68 trusts out of 304 in 2002) have been invited by the Government to tender to become legally independent organisations with stakeholder governance, in effect a type of Public Interest Company. At the time of publication 32 trusts had applied.

There are four key issues underlying the foundation trust policy: accountability, diversity, freedoms, and finance.

Accountability
The Secretary of State has positioned the foundation trust policy within the centre-left co-operative tradition, and much has been made of the stakeholder governance possible within these new trusts.

Anyone from the local community, anyone who has been a patient in the last three years, or anyone who is an employee of the trust will be able to register as a 'member'. Members will:

- have voting rights for the election of community members on a board of governors
- receive information about the performance of the foundation trust
- be consulted on the activities of the trust.

Members will be the formal owners of the trust and liable to pay a nominal sum of £1 in the event of insolvency. The assets of foundation trusts will be protected from demutualisation; members will receive no financial benefit from their involvement.

The board of governors will scrutinise the activity of the trust. In the absence of government Ministers they will be responsible for protecting the public interest. Trusts will be able to specify the size and composition of their governing body, but boards will have to consist of:

- representatives elected from the public membership
- people elected from the employee membership
- people nominated to represent partner organisations, such as PCTs and universities with ties to the trust

These governance arrangements could help tackle the long-criticised 'democratic deficit' in the NHS. There have traditionally been few mechanisms for involving patients and the public in the NHS. Community Health Councils were relatively weak and were abolished in the National Health Service Reform And Health Care Professions Act 2002. New Patients' Forums are being established to improve public involvement in PCTs and a Commission for Patient and Public Involvement in Health is being set up to monitor public involvement at a national level. Foundation trusts could help give patients and the public an even greater say over how local services are organised and delivered. However, it is not yet clear how these different mechanisms for increasing patient and public involvement in the NHS will work together. For example, how will the elected patient and public representatives on the board of foundation trusts relate to the local patient forums, to Primary Care Trusts or to the new powers of scrutiny of local government?

It is also possible that the effects and benefits of stakeholder governance have been overstated. It is not clear whether there will be real interest among the general public in becoming a member of the foundation trust, or in participating in the trust's board of governors. There is a danger that only those with the time and inclination will participate, excluding more vulnerable groups who arguably need health services the most. Whilst public governance of hospitals brings with it the possibility of greater openness in the NHS, it seems unlikely to result in the substantial increase in trust and accountability presumed by some devotees.

One potential advantage of the governance arrangements in foundation trusts is that they could help increase health practitioner's involvement in the management of the NHS. Many clinicians currently feel disengaged with the process of reform and that they are not given a sufficient say in how the NHS's priorities are set or where the extra money coming into the service is being invested. Recent evidence suggests that ensuring clinicians feel a sense of ownership over the process of change is critical to successful service reform (Gollop 2003). The stakeholder governance system of foundation trusts offers the potential to draw clinicians more effectively into the management of hospitals, which in turn could help reform services and improve health outcomes (Kendall and Lissauer 2003). However, it would also be a mistake to focus solely on involving consultants and clinicians: other NHS staff such as nurses and auxiliary staff also play a crucial role in the NHS and there is a good case for ensuring that they too are represented on any governance boards.

Although there are clear attractions in bridging the divide between clinicians and managers, there are also potential dangers. Given the power of consultants and the traditionally paternalistic relationship between doctors and patients there is a risk is that public members could become cheerleaders for trusts, rather than their scrutinisers.

Diversity

Foundation trusts are also part of a move to create greater diversity and contestability within the NHS, which the Government sees as crucial to improving the efficiency and quality of provision.

Contestability is the principle whereby new providers of services can be brought in to replace those who are not performing adequately. This acts as a continual incentive for providers to consider how they can improve their service. Contestability differs from the forced use of competition within public services in that there is no regular market testing. Instead, it provides a latent but real option that public managers can choose alternative providers if service quality slips. The principle of contestability can be applied within a publicly provided system. However, IPPR has argued that to date the public sector has suffered from too limited a pool of providers; too little diversity of provision (IPPR 2001).

The Government has signalled a willingness to encourage private and non-profit providers to deliver health services, alongside the traditional public ownership. For example, the Government signed a 'concordat' with the private sector in November 2000 in order to help access spare capacity within the private health system. In addition, new Diagnostic and Treatment Centres, some of which will be run by the private sector, will soon treat NHS patients needing routine elective surgery such as hip replacements.

The development of foundation trusts can be seen as part of the trend towards increasing diversity within the NHS. They provide non-state-owned options in an area where government may be unwilling to use for-profit providers. Government is reluctant to let privately-owned hospitals deliver complex clinical care for because it fears that contracts will be unable to safeguard the public interest (see Chapter 2). Undoubtedly, the Government is also attracted by the political benefits of a mutually-owned NHS, rather one owned by corporations.

The Government has also portrayed diversity in the NHS as a means of promoting greater patient choice. This is seen as vital if the NHS is to keep pace with wider changes in society, such as increasing consumerism. It is also seen as a good way to retain middle-class buy-in into the NHS. Pilot schemes to increase choice are already under way: patients waiting for more than six months in a number of areas already have some choice over where they are treated. From 2005 patients should be routinely offered choice at the point of GP referral (Department of Health 2002c).

Underpinning these moves to create more diversity, contestability and choice in the NHS is a strengthened purchaser-provider split. Seventy five per cent of NHS budgets now flow through the commissioning bodies, the Primary Care Trusts (Department of Health 2001). There has also been a little-noticed return to funding flows, whereby money is set to follow the patient through the use of new Health Resource Groups (HRGs). These will provide a fixed price for treatments, so providers will compete on productivity (and possibly ultimately quality), not on price as was the case under the Conservative Government's internal market (Department of Health 2002c). HRGs are to be introduced slowly, starting with key disease groups. The suggestion is that foundation trusts will implement more HRGs more quickly compared to traditional NHS trusts.

In order for this regulated market to work in the NHS, there needs to be a substantial degree of excess capacity. Without this the danger is that instead of commissioners choosing providers, the opposite might occur.

Freedoms

Another of the principle aims behind the foundation trust idea is the intention to reduce the bureaucracy and political intervention faced by local NHS trust managers from central government.

The Department of Health's *Guide to NHS Foundation Trusts* (2002b) suggests that foundation trusts will be free in law from the Secretary of State's current powers of direction. This could mean a reduction in the frequent NHS directives sent from Whitehall, and foundation trust managers may no longer have to seek Ministerial approval for routine decisions. The Department has also indicated that foundation trusts will receive some exemption from the detailed performance management regime that covers NHS trusts. It has been reported that trust managers are seeking exemption from all but nine of the 62 targets to which NHS trusts are currently subject (*Health Service Journal* 2003a). However, foundation trusts will still have to meet national standards as set out by various bodies, such as the National Institute for Clinical Excellence (NICE) and through National Service Frameworks. The extent to which foundation trusts will be genuinely exempt from central targets and directives is as yet unclear and likely to be a matter of fierce negotiation.

The Government has also suggested that foundation trusts will have the freedom to set local pay and conditions. This is a controversial decision. In a capacity constrained system such as the NHS, it could lead to inflated salaries. Critics of the foundation trust policy suggest it will result in a two-tier system with pay and conditions lagging behind in NHS trusts that have been unable to achieve the required three star status.

Foundation trusts are also likely to be given some additional financial freedoms, including the ability to retain income from land sales. However, it appears that requests by trust managers for freedoms to decide on their intake of private patients and for additional borrowing powers have (rightly) been resisted by government.

At the time of writing there is still little clarity about the practical extent of any freedoms that foundation trusts will enjoy. Indeed, NHS trust managers have accused the Government of watering down their initial intentions (especially regarding private patients and freedoms to borrow) in order to pacify Labour backbenchers (*Health Service Journal* 2003b). Government has good reason to restrict these particular freedoms. However, it is too soon to tell whether the Government will actually allow foundation trusts the type of management freedoms their rhetoric has implied.

Finance
Throughout 2002 the Treasury appeared cautious about foundation trusts, particularly about the prospect that they might be given unrestricted access to the private finance markets.

At least in the early days of the foundation trust policy, the prospect of getting investment 'off balance sheet' was a prime concern for supporters of the policy, since this gave the appearance of permitting higher departmental spending without falling foul of Treasury spending limits. Although, controversially, the Treasury has been happy to justify the PFI for this reason, they rightly dismissed the 'off balance sheet' case for foundation trusts. In any case, if the state was to bear the financial risk for foundation trusts it would be highly unlikely that they would be judged off balance sheet by the Office for National Statistics. The 'off balance sheet' case for taxpayer-funded public private partnerships, including PICs, is poor (see page 70). However, if PICs remain on-balance sheet, there is even less reason to use private finance from the point of view of individual government departments.

Using private finance in foundation trusts would leave institutions facing higher costs of finance than they could receive via government, without the usual benefits. For example, risk would continue to be borne by the Government, and as discussed on page 58, lenders are unlikely to provide a similar degree of corporate governance as that provided by shareholders.

A more suitable alternative for foundation trusts might be the kind of prudential borrowing framework currently being developed for local government (see page 73). On the other hand, some have argued that foundation trusts will suffer from creeping government control if they are not given absolute control over their own investment decisions, a fate suffered by the NHS trusts established by the Conservative Government in the early 1990s. If prudential frameworks maintain central government's (and especially the Treasury's) right to dictate how investment is spent this will be a fair criticism. However, prudential frameworks do not necessarily have to mean continued Whitehall intervention in local priorities.

The suggestion that foundation trusts should be opposed because they will lead to runaway government borrowing is mistaken. The Government is right to seek to control overall levels of public investment, and is right to prevent foundation trusts from having the freedom to increase their levels of debt to whatever level they desire. A borrowing free-for-all would adversely affect the stability of the Government's finances, and any poor investment decisions would fall to the Government to repay, not the private sector. The use of centrally determined prudential borrowing frameworks is one answer to this problem. However, even if private finance were used, regulation, perhaps through the new 'NHS Bank' could prevent foundation trusts from incautious borrowing.[5] Indeed, the new NHS Bank might eventually play a similar role to the Housing Finance Corporation and Education Capital Finance, in acting as a funding intermediary to help develop a private sector market in health financing.

Criticisms of foundation trust reforms
One of the biggest critics of the foundation trust policy is the former Labour Secretary of State for Health, Frank Dobson MP. His principle concern is that foundation trust status will only be available to the best NHS trusts and this could lead to the development of a two-tier system, for example through different staff pay and conditions. However, two-tierism is not a consequence of the foundation trust principle, instead it is a result of the way in which the Government intends to introduce the policy. The Government has indicated that over time more trusts should have access to foundation status. It argues that restricting early participants to three star trusts will provide a useful incentive for poorer trusts to improve. The Government is also concerned about the ability of poorer performing trusts to improve without a tough regime of targets and monitoring. It is also understandably cautious about introducing another substantial structural change to the NHS.

Although there may be benefits of the foundation trust system in encouraging more co-operation between clinicians and managers, by fostering more competition between health providers the new system might make co-operation between professionals working in separate institutions more difficult. It may also make co-ordinated strategic planning in the NHS more complex.

Another criticism of the way in which the Government has approached NHS reform is that it appears to have spent more time and effort investigating PIC status for hospitals than in getting the delicate balance of the new funding mechanism in the NHS right. The success of the new NHS will arguably rely more on the payment mechanism rewarding quality and capacity than on the levels of public involvement in hospital governance (Palmer 2003).

A missed opportunity?
It is arguable that the principle of foundation trusts might be better applied to Primary Care Trusts. Improving public involvement over the way services are commissioned is as, if not more, important as giving local communities a greater say in how services are provided. The Department of Health proposed foundation status for PCTs in their document 'Delivering the NHS plan' in April 2002, but

there appears to have been little active development of this idea during the intervening period.

Improving public accountability over the commissioning process could help readdress the democratic balance between the commissioners and providers of health services. This might help reduce the potential for 'producer capture'. However, more significantly, it could reduce the potential for public opposition to PCTs that moved funding away from a local hospital in order to provide a wider choice of health providers for their local health populations. If democratic pressure is applied to PCTs to just commission from their local trust then the nascent regulated market in health care is unlikely to succeed. Even if PCTs were to have community ownership, there would remain a democratic tension between the 'mutual' ownership of health providers (the Trusts) and PCTs who are tasked with providing care on behalf of their local populations.

Conclusion

Foundation trusts have the potential to provide two key advantages. First, they could improve efficiency within the NHS as result of implementing a stronger purchaser/provider split and by reducing centrally imposed bureaucracy. Secondly, by bringing in a hitherto unseen degree of openness and direct accountability in the NHS they could help reconnect the public with the NHS and help bring about a more patient-focussed service.

There are signs that the Government is keen to use the foundation trust idea into a range of different services, such as new Children's Trusts which bring together all services for children. However, as this report has made clear, the PIC concept must be applied cautiously on a case by case basis. There are dangers in over-applying a new policy idea.

The test of the foundation trust policy will be how far the Minister's rhetoric about devolving power and responsibility is matched by the reality. There will remain a strong line of influence from the Secretary of State down to Chief Executives of NHS foundation trusts. Likewise, it will be easy for Ministers to continue to exert control through the commissioning side of health care and through the strict application of national standards. Given the history of the NHS, the Government will have to overcome substantial scepticism from managers, clinicians and the public before their announcements about devolution of power are taken at face value.

Dealing with risks in Public Interest Companies

This chapter has set out six ways in which risks in Public Interest Companies can be managed in the absence of equity. It now turns to each of these in more detail. Dealing with risk is one of the most important issues for a potential Public Interest Company. Without clarity on risk a Public Interest Company will face a difficult and uncertain future.

Equity is a tried and tested method of dealing with and pricing risk. These alternatives whilst adequate are generally less well understood and less well suited to coping with risk. As a result, PICs are probably more suitable to low risk environments.

1. Lenders could bear the risks

Lenders do not bear risks like shareholders. In fact, in order to lend to an organisation debt issuers will expect that the great majority of risks are dealt with by other parties. This makes the likelihood that they would bear all financial risks in a Public Interest Company remote.

Lenders have a range of attitudes towards risk, dependent upon the type of debt they are issuing. Not all debt is typical low margin senior debt. For example, subordinated debt acts very much like equity: in cases of bankruptcy lenders only receive their payment after typical (senior) debt is paid off. As a result it attracts a higher return than senior debt. The important difference between equity and subordinated debt is that this debt does not provide dividend payments and does not confer ownership rights.

So could subordinated debt be used in the place of equity? Clearly, subordinated debt has an important role to play in the financing of Public Interest Companies. For example, Glas Cymru has many tranches of debt, from triple-A rated bonds that are backed by monoline credit insurers through to unrated bonds that bear significantly higher risk. Subordinated debt could be used to entirely replace equity, or it could be used as part of a package of measures alongside other types of risk management. However, convincing lenders that they should bear any such risk is likely to be difficult.

In addition, lenders are likely to demand similar rights of control over an organisation as equity investors if they are to bear similar risk; rights such as consultation on major projects and rights to hire and fire the board. If lenders were given the same rights as shareholders in a Public Interest Company such organisations could lose the presumed benefits of stakeholder membership and therefore an important advantage of PIC status.

Lenders providing subordinated risk should also be presumed to price risk appropriately, leading to an overall cost of finance at least the same as in a traditionally financed organisation. Indeed, given most lenders dislike of managing risks and their inexperience in doing so, it is likely that they would price their overall cost of finance higher than in a typically financed organisation.

2. Sufficient cash reserves can be built up over the short term to absorb expected future risks

This scenario is possible only where an organisation can be sure to build up enough surpluses in its early years to cope with any subsequent financial shocks. A PIC needs to be confident that these shocks will not appear before the surplus is accumulated. Therefore, as a first consideration, whilst this approach has been used before it is unlikely to be successful where the PIC is immediately exposed to ongoing risks which it is difficult to control (such as significant demand risk).

Surpluses can be generated with a good deal of certainty where revenue is subject to regulation and the investment requirement is lower than regulated or market value. This unusual situation applies to Glas Cymru, the Public Interest Company created to take over the Welsh Water domestic water utility business from Western Power Distribution (WPD) in 2001. However, it is an unusual case, unlikely to be easily replicated.

Another situation where equity-like surpluses can be achieved is when revenue comes from contracts with the public sector. The Government could help build up surpluses by agreeing to pay over the odds in the early years of the contract in order to build up equity-like reserves in the organisations. In this case the surpluses do not result from any inherent lower costs of a Public Interest Company, but instead are effectively being contributed by the public sector. This is really a variation of the 'financial support' example, which is discussed next.

Case study 6: Glas Cymru

Glas Cymru was, in effect, a management buy out of the privatised welsh water company Dwr Cymru, previously owned by Hyder (which in turn was bought by Western Power Distribution in 2000). Glas Cymru is organised as a Company Limited by Guarantee.

The main driver behind Glas' transformation to a Public Interest Company was not any considerations about accountability or stakeholder involvement. Instead it was a business decision about how best to deliver water services at highest quality and lowest cost. The political benefits to Glas of being a Public Interest Company were clearly secondary to these financial benefits.

Glas delivers water and sewage services in Wales. It is a monopoly essential service. Moreover, the water industry is a naturally stable business, and heavily capital intensive. As a result of this capital programme, the costs of finance for water utilities have a significant impact on the total costs of the business. Those involved in putting together the Glas deal set out to undercut the water sector's cost of capital by putting in place a number of arrangements designed to reveal and then 'lock in' the fact that a regulated water and sewerage business is low risk and could be financed and managed as such. Their aim was to reduce Welsh Water's cost of financing assets below the sector's cost of capital by reducing risk and dealing with investor concerns about risk. They would then use these savings to build up financial reserves in the company, which would act as an equity buffer.

Glas Cymru has sought to minimise risks in a number of ways:

- It became a single purpose company, preventing itself from diversifying into non-regulatory activities. Following water privatisation, shareholder water utilities were keen to diversify as this offered the prospects of higher profits outside regulated activities. However, these profits have not materialised, and 'diversification risk' is now built into the costs of capital of shareholder owned water utilities.

- Glas embarked on substantial competitive outsourcing, with over 80 per cent of Glas' annual expenditure now carried out by third parties (Burns 2003). This has transferred risk onto external private companies. This process of competitive contracting also helps reduce regulatory risk caused by the regulator inaccurately predicting the costs of various activities.

- Glas incentivises good management. The water industry is a highly measurable business, unlike healthcare and other public services. Directors are incentivised through bonus schemes to both increase financial reserves, and to improve customer services and environmental impacts (see page 30)

- Glas has strong corporate governance. Glas is fortunate to have a highly able majority group of non-executive directors on its board. Lenders are also conscious that their capital is 'at risk' and have stronger than normal step-in rights should company performance deteriorate. In addition, the monoline insurance company MBIA plays an even more active role in corporate governance. Behind all this there are also 50 public members of Glas who hold the board to account.

Building up financial reserves is crucial to the success of Glas. It is able to do this because of two key factors. Firstly, it paid less than market value for Welsh Water, and therefore only needed to issue bonds covering around 95 per cent of the value of the business. This provided a sufficient equity-like buffer to protect Welsh Water from adverse financial shocks in the early days of the business.

Secondly, Glas is seeking to increase this buffer zone to 15 per cent of its regulatory asset base by the end of the current regulatory price control period, and by the end of 2002 had already built up a surplus of some £350 million. Glas is able to increase these reserves because of the financing efficiency it has secured through undercutting the cost of capital set for the industry by OFWAT. For the current regulatory period 2000-2005 the cost of capital in real terms was set at 6.5 per cent and Glas Cymru issued bonds which secured a cost of finance in real terms of around 4.5 per cent, a saving of over £50 million annually or over 10 per cent of Welsh Water's annual revenues. Glas Cymru's bonds have trading strongly since the £1.9 billion issue in May 2001, demonstrating continued investor support for the new structure and indicating the potential for significant further savings in the years ahead as Welsh Water continues to fund its large capital investment programme.

Glas has been able to eliminate the conflict of interests between shareholders and users of its services, whereby shareholders have little inherent interest in producing high quality services and low prices for customers. In Glas, lenders and customers both have an interest in seeing Glas build up reserves, as this creates a virtuous circle: it reduces risks for lenders, which improves credit quality, which lowers the costs of capital, which reduces prices.

3. Financial support can be obtained from taxpayers as a substitute for risk capital

Contingent funding arrangements, where the Government provides loans to be drawn upon in times of need, have been used recently to support Network Rail. An alternative method, although arguably less cash flow efficient, would be to fund the reserve by grant, or by over-funding a provider though higher than normal contract payments.

A government guarantee is an effective way to deal with risk in a Public Interest Company from the company's perspective. It is likely to make lenders happy to provide finance, as the Government will not break its commitment if the organisation fails. However, government itself, particularly the Treasury, is likely to be rather less enthusiastic.

A key problem is that this option fails to transfer any financial risk to the private sector, negating one of the key justifications for using private finance in PPPs. If projects get into difficulty it will be the Government who is called on to provide extra funds, and the private debt providers will be amongst the first in line to receive their payments. Also, because the Public Interest Company is borrowing money from the private debt markets, rather than borrowing via the Treasury itself, the costs of borrowing will be higher.

The only other reason for the Government to use private finance after having accepted financial risk is because any investment may appear 'off balance sheet', which can appear to offer advantages to individual government departments. As discussed on page 70, 'off balance sheet' justifications for PPPs including PICs and PFIs are not valid for taxpayer-funded public services. Indeed, if financial risk remains with the Government it makes it likely that taxpayer-funded services will actually remain on the Government's balance sheet even if provided by a PIC. In these situations private finance will come at extra cost compared to direct government borrowing, but will bring none of the usual advantages such as a mechanism to deal with risk and a source of effective corporate governance.

There are also potential political problems in using financial support as a substitute for risk capital in public services funded through taxation. If the Government agreed to build up financial reserves for a general public service Public Interest Company the Government would see their scarce resources being used to support a structural form rather than being used to directly improve those services. This is unlikely to be popular with a government that has based its reputation on improving public services within a few short years, nor with the public that might feel the money should be spent on the front line and not remain within the bank accounts of public organisations.

It has been argued that government cannot provide public institutions with the freedom to manage their organisations properly without providing them with the freedom to borrow. However, giving a PIC the freedom to borrow is not the same thing as allowing it the freedom to borrow from the private sector. It is possible – perhaps even preferable – for taxpayer funded PICs to have freedom over their own investment decisions, but for this finance to come via the Government rather than the private sector direct. The prudential borrowing frameworks being considered for local government is a possible way forward (see page 73).

The Government will have to calculate whether the extra costs and difficulties of providing an equity-like buffer for PICs are worth the extra management freedoms and efficiencies that may flow from a new regime. It may be that the potential efficiency savings from working on a contracting basis for public services outweighs the extra risks shouldered by government.

Case study 7: British Energy

British Energy is the privatised company responsible for the operation of the UK's nuclear power stations and a number of coal-fired power stations. A 25 per cent over-capacity in UK electricity generation and the introduction of the New Electricity Trading Arrangements (NETA) led to 40 per cent drop in wholesale prices between 1998 and 2003. As a result of these reduced prices, high fixed costs (partly as a result of expensive reprocessing contracts with British Nuclear Fuels Limited) and sheer bad luck in having two of its nuclear reactors out of service, British Energy in early 2003 is struggling to compete with other sources of electricity generation.

British Energy produces around 20 per cent of the UK's electricity in 2002. To prevent a shortfall in electricity revenue and for other strategic reasons the Government is reluctant to let the privatised organisation go bankrupt. As a result government provided £650 million in loans in 2002, and promised even more financial help to keep the shareholder-owned company operating.

However, the Government is rightly worried about the current organisational form of British Energy. It learned from the Railtrack experience that shareholders in essential services that are reliant on heavy subsidy are adept at extracting extra subsidies from government rather than improving the efficiency and management of their business. Like Railtrack, British Energy was eager to provide dividend payments to shareholders even when the company was in financial difficulty. Also, whilst the management of British Energy has not been criticised in the same way as the management of Railtrack, the shareholders that control British Energy have not been entirely responsible in ensuring that the long-term costs of the business will be met. For example, the company does not have enough funding set aside to decommission its nuclear power stations, should this be necessary as a result of market changes.

As a result, the Government is considering turning British Energy into a PIC. But would this provide a solution to the company's problems?

Shareholders are interested in the short-term value of the company, and so transferring British Energy to a solely debt-financed PIC could bring benefits of better long-term vision (see page 81). However, if it was to become a Public Interest Company the Government needs to be clear that it would be called on to bear the risks of the organisation, and these risks are substantial (although it could be argued that the final risks remained with the Government anyway, even when the company was privatised).

Shareholders in British Energy have been happy to bear the upside of their risks. They should also be made to pay for the downsides. It is unacceptable for British Energy shareholders to be insured against the risks of the business through government support. Instead, the Government should be prepared to allow British Energy to become bankrupt and then to set up a new organisation, without shareholders. This could help protect the public purse if subsidies are required, and the long-term vision of bondholders could be better suited to this type of business.

The key issues that have resulted in British Energy being in this position are not linked to the failings of the organisational structure of management, as arguably they were for Railtrack. Instead it is the wider competitive market for electricity that has caused these problems. Before making any decision government needs to decide what the problem is for British Energy: is there a competitive market for electricity, or does the Government believe it should have nuclear energy generation regardless of the costs? Only if it is the latter does PIC status for British Energy become a serious option. Even so, the fact that British Energy is not a natural monopoly means that PIC status is less attractive than it might otherwise be.

Public Interest Company status for British Energy might help protect the taxpayer should continued subsidy be required, but it will not on its own repair the company's fortunes make it a self-supporting entity once again. Public Interest Company status is an option, but it is not a solution for the problems of British Energy.

4. Risks could be transferred on to the users of the service: the Consumer Service Corporation

This model is only useful in a very small number of cases, but where it is applicable it is perhaps the most effective way of organising a Public Interest Company. This model is such a specialised and effective type of Public Interest Company it is useful to refer to it as a sub-category: the *Consumer Service Corporation* (McCallum 2002).

Consumer Service Corporations work by effectively turning the users of the service into the owners of the organisation that delivers that service. It gives those users key rights over governance, and users assume the equity-like risk.

This method of dealing with risk in a Public Interest Company is only applicable for monopoly essential public enterprises. It only works for public enterprises because users of the service need to bear the direct financial cost of payment, and it only works for monopoly essential services because users will not accept higher charges if they can receive these services elsewhere or can do without the service at all.

To work, Consumer Service Corporations need to be subject to a number of qualifying restrictions. First, it is vital that in a Public Interest Company where users bear risk there is clarity that this is the case. If users are at risk from large increases in prices for services resulting from poor management decisions then all interested parties (including users, the Government, management and debt lenders) have to be clear where these risks lie. Secondly, users need to be effective governors of the organisation, with probably a financial interest in the success of the organisation. It is not clear whether the general public would be sufficiently incentivised to fulfil this crucial governance role (see page 38).

Consumer Service Corporations can align the interests of management with the interests of users. When it works, the Consumer Service Corporation eliminates the natural pricing conflict generally found between a monopoly corporation and its consumers, whereby the corporation wants to charge high rates to maximise profits and consumers want to pay low rates to minimise expenditures. With the pricing conflict removed, the Consumer Service Corporation will find its interests fundamentally aligned with those of its users. As a result, it can achieve high overall efficiency.

Case study 8: Nav Canada

Nav Canada is the company responsible for running air traffic control in Canada. It is constituted as a Non-Share Capital Corporation, which is a legal form used to deliver a variety of utility-type public services in Canada. It is a good example of a Consumer Service Corporation, a specific type of Public Interest Company which is largely, but not necessarily completely, run by the consumers of its own services.

Nav Canada has been in operation since 1996, and has been a success. It has introduced complex new computer systems, reduced user charge rates by 35 per cent, substantially improved safety and service levels and in 2001 won the prestigious Eagle Award as the world's best air traffic control system, from the international user group IATA.

Nav Canada has good credit rating scores of AA+ from Standard & Poor's and Aa2 from Moody's. It has practically unlimited access to debt capital at one of the lowest costs of any Canadian corporate issuer; resulting in a pre-tax cost of funds at around one third lower than that of high quality Canadian share-based utilities. Because airlines bear the financial risks in Nav Canada, bondholders were not even affected by the downturn in business after the terrorist attacks on America on September 11th 2001; it was the only aviation company in Canada that Moody's did not put on credit watch after the attacks.

The users of Nav Canada, the airlines, are prominent Members in Nav Canada and have the power to appoint a substantial number of Directors. As a result there is no need for a government appointed regulator to protect these interests separately. Nav Canada is free to vary the prices of its services without intervention from an independent price regulator (highly unusual for a monopoly enterprise).

Consumer Service Corporations operating as Public Interest Companies in essential monopoly services have serious implications for the regulation of these services. Typically, enterprises that provide a public service and charge users direct are subject to a privatise/regulate model of provision when not provided by government itself. The need for regulation is obvious; without it the shareholder organisation could exploit the public to improve their profits by providing poor quality essential services at a high cost.

In the case of a Consumer Service Corporation, the users of the service operate effective control over the organisation, eliminating the conflict between owners and users. In such circumstances there is no longer a role for traditional price regulation, although there will still be a place for safety or environmental regulation. Price regulation might remain in a new guise to ensure an equitable distribution of prices to all users, as not all users might be represented as controlling members.

Indeed, Consumer Service Corporations could be effective where there is a minority of corporate user interests which display essential qualities for good corporate governance, but where many (perhaps domestic) customers do not. A new style price regulator could set a formula that set out the proportion of prices to be borne by each group, and then leave the Consumer Service Corporation to raise or lower prices in accordance with this pre-set formula.

In monopoly essential services one of the main business risks is regulatory risk, and as we have witnessed in the UK water industry, the impact of regulatory risk can be significant. Equity-based private companies delivering monopoly services create a need for price regulation to protect consumers against the shareholders' profit motives. Price regulation in turn creates a need for share capital, as a buffer to protect lenders from the initial impact of any negative regulatory action. We have a self-reinforcing circle in which equity creates the need for regulation, which in turn creates the need for equity (McCallum 2002).

Consumer Service Corporations break the circle. Because there are no private sector shareholders, price regulation is no longer needed to the same degree; and if price regulation is adjusted appropriately, nor is equity capital needed to protect lenders. But both steps must be taken to gain the full advantage. If we simply switch from an equity-based enterprise to a Consumer Service Corporation, without adjusting the manner in which prices are regulated, then lenders' continued exposure to regulatory risk will unnecessarily reduce management flexibility and increase the cost of funds. Glas Cymru has found itself in this position; the public interest is being protected by both its stakeholder governance as well as through the water regulator OFWAT. It would make more sense for the water regulator to take a different position in relation to Glas Cymru, and eventually allow it to set its own prices. Such a role-reducing proposition is unlikely to be welcomed by OFWAT, however.

By eliminating traditional regulatory risk from monopoly essential services, the Consumer Service Corporation in effect provides a new environment for the organisation. This can have a positive effect on the costs of capital for the business (see page 74).

There are few monopoly essential services. However, this model could be used to deliver utility services such as air traffic control, water and sewerage services, and electricity and gas distribution.

Case study 9: Electricity distribution

Using a Public Interest Company to control electricity distribution is a possibility already being lobbied for in Northern Ireland (Cardew & Co 2002). The driver behind the change is that the costs of electricity are much higher than on the British mainland, which is a significant problem for energy-intensive manufacturing businesses. A group of such users are arguing for a change, claiming that they have sufficient financial interest in the electricity market to act as good governors. They will clearly depend on a reliable electricity supply and have a real incentive to reduce costs.

Such a system has much to recommend it. If the PIC was free to set its own prices then it could also usefully benefit from a cheaper cost of capital, although regulation would still be needed to ensure that there was an equitable distribution of prices between corporate and domestic users. The fact that there is both one electricity supply company (Northern Ireland Electricity) and a separate regulator in Northern Ireland from the rest of the UK (The Office for the Regulation of Electricity and Gas) mean that this approach is potentially more likely to occur than on the UK mainland. If it does happen it will serve as a useful test case for the rest of the UK (Director General for Electricity Supply 2002)

However, another solution to the same problems in Northern Ireland Electricity would be to open the market to increased competition. IPPR's recent pamphlet on utility regulation argues that competition within a PLC model might be a first best option, with PIC models considered only if regulation and competition are unable to secure desired outcomes (Corry 2003).

---

5. Risks can be absorbed within the operational performance of the company

This option is rarely consciously employed as the sole mechanism to deal with risk, although in practice it can often feature as a partial solution. It depends on there being significant cost savings to be realised from the organisation's performance.

Good managers of Public Interest Companies will seek to realise these cost savings from day one (potentially using these savings to create a surplus discussed above). In fact it may be more difficult to manage such cost-saving changes to the organisation in times of financial distress. Relying on cost savings alone is a very risky way to cope with risk.

Nevertheless, many Public Interest Companies will have been transferred from public ownership, where there are relatively few efficiency drivers. As a result, financial distress may well provide an incentive to extract additional cost savings.

6. Risks can be externalised, through outsourced contracts or insurance

As we have discussed, lenders will assume little or no risk in an organisation. The strategies outlined above demonstrate how these risks can be borne in alternative ways to equity. However, if an organisation bears little or no residual risk then lenders may be willing to lend without the presence of equity.

Some businesses are inherently low risk. The water and sewage industry is an inherently stable and predictable industry and regulatory risk is one of the most prominent risks. Glas Cymru seeks to minimise these low risks further by structuring itself as a management company, with all its operations carried out under sub-contracts with external private companies. These sub-contracts work in a very similar way to traditional PFI contracts, although have shorter contract periods. The contractor takes on a significant degree of operational risk; if the output specifications in the contracts are not met the private contractor bears the costs. Through the use of sub-contracts Glas is left with very low levels of risk within its core business.

Another similar method to reduce residual risk is to use monoline insurance. This is where a company insures its ability to pay back lenders. By insuring for any remaining risk within an organisation a Public Interest Company can externalise these risks and provide the guarantees needed for lenders to be confident that their debt will be repaid. Glas also used insurance to externalise some of its remaining risks.

The use of sub-contracting and insurance both involve paying for others to take on the equity risks of a business. These equity risks are transferred to private companies with their own equity base. The use of equity has not been eliminated here, instead it has been transferred. In some ways this means that Public Interest Companies using these methods are still reliant on 'profit'. In most cases the fact that shareholders are one step removed from the core management process means they do not exert the same influence over the business. But if contracts are used to externalise key elements of the public service, as they are in the 'not-for-profit PFIs' then there may be no justification for using a PIC at all: the dangers of incomplete contracts will remain.

Case study 10: National Air Traffic Services (NATS)

National Air Traffic Services (NATS), the company responsible for air traffic control in the United Kingdom, is a peculiar organisation which has evolved into its present PIC-like form more by luck than judgement.

In the months preceding the 1997 general election the Labour opposition were accused of having a 'black hole' in their finances by the Conservative Government because Labour had not matched a Conservative pledge to privatise NATS. The Labour Party diffused a difficult political situation by proposing a public private partnership for NATS, even though there had been no thinking about how or why this would be done. The PPP was included in the Labour Government's Transport Act 2000.

This PPP was more of a part-privatisation than a typical partnership scheme. In it, price and safety regulation would be carried out by the independent Civil Aviation Authority (CAA), whilst government would set out its requirements for NATS in a strategic partnership arrangement, a type of contract. Meanwhile, NATS itself would become a joint-venture company; government would have a 49 per cent shareholding underpinned by 'golden share' powers, a consortium of private airline companies would be the lead partner with 46 per cent of shares, and staff would hold the remaining five per cent.

The proposal was highly controversial. Criticisms centred around the introduction of the profit motive in a monopoly essential service where safety was the primary purpose of the business (House of Commons 2000). Despite the joint-venture arrangement, regulating such an entity and ensuring the public interest through the strategic partnership arrangement would be difficult.

In the end the market itself resolved the problem. The customers of NATS, the airlines, formed a consortium which bid and won the NATS contract. Doing so made NATS an unusual organisation. It was a PPP, a part-privatisation, a joint venture, and now it was also a Public Interest Company, or more accurately a Consumer Service Corporation (see page 64). NATS' PIC-like tendency was confirmed when the airline group announced that they would operate the business on a 'not for commercial return' basis. Although they never explained what was meant by this the implication was clear – at least in the short term and on a voluntary basis they would not seek dividend payments from their investment in NATS.

Perhaps not surprisingly given its history, the final structure of NATS was not well thought through and contained a number of flaws. The principle problem was that there was no flexibility by which NATS could cope with risk. The shareholders had become investors for strategic, not financial reasons and would not bear risks like typical shareholders. However, NATS had no other method of dealing with risk in place. Just after the new NATS had been established in summer 2001 the terrorist attacks on New York and Washington, compounded by the downturn in the world economy, left it struggling to cope with falling income and high debt. It was forced to deal with risk by finding efficiency improvements in the organisation, despite managers being new and the organisation undergoing substantial organisational change anyway. It was a risky way to cope with risk.

Government did not want to bail out NATS, especially as the PPP had been up and running for such a short amount of time. They tried to persuade the airline group to put in more equity, but the companies were not interested for two reasons. Firstly, they too were struggling financially in the post-September 11th environment. Secondly, they had invested for strategic not financial reasons. They had already purchased their influence and they were not expecting financial returns on their investment. In the end the Government did provide additional equity and it also persuaded British Airports Authority (BAA) to enter the deal as an additional equity investor.

NATS is still searching for a lasting solution. Its immediate balance sheet problems have been eased, but the Government and the CAA remain seemingly unconscious to the possibilities of NATS' peculiar organisational structure. As a Consumer Service Corporation NATS is in a position to take charge of its own pricing levels. The CAA should retain a role ensuring both safety and that equity exists between operators in the way in which pricing is set, but there is no need for an economic regulator to second-guess the needs of users when those users actually direct the company in question.

The airlines not represented in the airline consortia are suspicious about giving NATS freedom over pricing, and have supported the CAA's stance. This is primarily due to the fact that the airline group are equity investors in NATS, and might be seen to have a conflict of interests between acting in the interests of the industry and protecting their own investments. There is a strong case for reorganising NATS along the lines of Nav Canada, so that the airlines (and staff and government) retain their influence but are not equity investors. Indeed, if NATS was in charge of its own pricing levels then there would be no need for equity as risk would be transferred onto the users, the airlines themselves.

The final advantage of such a change in NATS' structure is that by eliminating the CAA's role in regulating price a significant element of regulatory risk would also be avoided. This could have a beneficial influence on NATS' costs of capital.

Other financial issues for Public Interest Companies— balance sheet issues

Discussions of Public Interest Companies in the media, the House of Commons and elsewhere have made much of their presumed 'off balance sheet' accounting treatment. However, as with other PPPs, balance sheet justifications for using taxpayer-funded PICs are entirely bogus.

What are 'balance sheet' issues?

The Government, like any major organisation, is required to list its income and expenditure in order to make clear the state of the nation's finances. Spending by non-government organisations, such as private business or charities is obviously not included in the Government's accounts. However, there are some organisations that are difficult to classify as either private or government. For example, Public Private

Partnerships where the organisation delivering the public service is a private company, but where the payments to fund the organisation come from directly from the Government. Public Interest Companies that are a hybrid type of organisation are even more difficult to assess.

People are concerned about the accounting treatment of these intermediate organisations because:

- if organisations are counted as being on the Government's balance sheet this can appear to limit the amount the Government can spend in other areas

- if organisations are counted as off the Government's balance sheet these organisations have the freedoms enjoyed by other private sector companies to borrow from the financial markets without Government restrictions

The Government is right to look at the amount it is borrowing and spending in order to achieve economic stability. Its 'sustainable investment rule': that the proportion of Public Sector Net Debt to GDP should remain within a prudent 40 per cent limit is an arbitrary but well supported target.

Balance sheet issues and the PFI

The Private Finance Initiative (PFI) was launched in 1992 under Conservative Chancellor Norman Lamont. The fact that most PFIs were judged to be off the Government's balance sheet was the PFI's major attraction, particularly at a time when a key priority was to reduce the budget deficit that had increased sharply in the early 1990s recession.

The PFI appeared to offer 'extra' investment by bringing in private finance for public capital projects. Government departments saw that if they used the PFI for major capital deals then their existing capital budget from the Treasury would stay intact, allowing 'additional' projects to get the go-ahead. The Labour government has hailed the PFI as facilitating its ambitious hospital building programme and other capital-intensive projects.

This 'off balance sheet' justification for the PFI is discredited. There is clearly no real 'extra' investment. The private sector only raises the finance to invest on the Governments behalf, and the Government – or rather the taxpayer – has to fund all of the costs of the service over the lifetime of the deal. Although the Treasury and many leading politicians now (rightly) emphasise that 'value for money' decisions should be behind PFI deals, some leading Government Ministers and commentators still use 'off balance sheet' justifications for the PFI. Indeed, balance sheet issues remain an important driver behind many PPP deals.

Balance sheet issues and Public Interest Companies

As with the PFI, the accounting treatment of PICs has dominated discussions because of the superficial appeal of 'off balance sheet financing'. However, for taxpayer-funded PICs these arguments are similarly redundant. All borrowing by taxpayer-funded PICs remains a liability of the taxpayer. Judgements about what the Government can afford to borrow should not be skewed by whether this borrowing is or is not included in the Government's accounts.

The position of *public enterprise* PICs is more complex. Because these public enterprises will be wholly or partly funded by user charges rather than out of taxation, they are more likely to be judged to be off the Government's balance sheet. Calculations as to whether they are or are not included in the Government's accounts will be much more difficult, as has been seen in arguments over the accounting treatment of Network Rail (House of Commons 2003).

However, judging PICs (and other PPPs) on the basis of their accounting treatment is an odd way to arrive at the most appropriate way to organise a public service. The Government should be aiming for the best quality at the least cost for taxpayers. Starting from questions as to how these organisations are to be accounted for is unlikely to achieve the optimal result. Only when the optimal solution has been reached should the Government consider how the body should be accounted for.

There is a good argument for saying that government needs to rethink how it accounts for PPPs. For taxpayer-funded PPPs (including PICs) they should remove the dubious attractions that come with 'off balance sheet' status by always accounting for them as if they were on the Government's balance sheet. Meanwhile, for public enterprises (including public enterprise PICs) there may be some scope for reflecting the hybrid nature of these organisations in the Government's accounts, rather than insisting that bodies are simply either public or private and accounted for accordingly.

Prudential borrowing regimes

In typical companies it is shareholders who provide both risk capital and corporate governance. Lenders provide little of either. As discussed throughout this paper, despite the absence of shareholders in PICs, it is likely that lenders will not significantly change their role. Therefore, besides the dubious attractions of 'off balance sheet' accounting, what might private finance offer for taxpayer-funded PICs?

The answer is not a lot. Indeed, it may just result in higher costs of capital. Therefore, public sources of finance might be more appropriate for these types of PICs.

The Government is considering so-called 'prudential borrowing regimes' for local authorities and the Northern Ireland Assembly. Local authority airports were given these powers during the previous parliament. The prudential framework will put the focus on whether public authorities have the revenue base to sustain their capital expenditure programmes.

Critically, because local authorities and the Northern Ireland Assembly have tax raising powers, the risks associated with projects such as capital programmes that turn out to be more costly will be borne by local taxpayers rather than the Treasury. Risk is transferred from the general taxpayer to the local taxpayer. This would not be the case for NHS foundation trusts, which is likely to make a prudential regime less attractive to the Treasury.

However, it is arguable that a prudential regime is still useful for foundation trusts and other similar taxpayer-funded PICs on the basis that it combines the benefits of cheaper costs of capital, with regulated devolution. For example, the framework would be a simple way for central government to control overall investment in the NHS, without having continued direct control over specific spending plans. Where PICs did not have recourse to revenue raising powers this would, though, reduce the financial accountability of that organisation.

The prudential regime should reduce the incentives for 'off balance sheet' financing and help create a more level playing field between the PFI and other investment options. Overall, this principle should be considered more widely for financing taxpayer-funded PICs.

Secure income streams

In order for a Public Interest Company to obtain any private finance it is necessary for it to demonstrate a secure income stream. Regardless of questions over the total risk in the business and questions of how residual risk will be dealt with, lenders will want to ensure that there is income which will enable its interest and principal to be repaid. This will more often than not involve a long-term contract with the public sector (although direct user charges in an essential service are another source).

Not all Public Interest Companies have such guarantees; for example, many smaller scale PICs will be reliant on grant funding, and may provide a non-essential public service. A good example are some of the ex-local authority leisure centres which now operate PICs, for example Greenwich Leisure. Many of these organisations have been operationally successful. However, there remain questions about PIC leisure companies' inability to secure private investment because of their reliance on year-to-year grant funding from the local council (alongside user charges). Such investment may well be necessary if PICs are to maintain their advantage in what is a competitive market with other private sector leisure providers (4Ps 2001).

Is debt financing cheaper than equity financing?

In a typically financed company that uses a mixture of equity and debt, the cost of debt is significantly lower than the cost of equity. This begs the question as to whether an organisation financed solely by debt will have lower overall costs of finance. If it does then this would be a significant advantage for PICs over traditionally financed entities. Such claims have often been made in favour of PICs (Grayling 2002; OFREG 2001).

The starting point for a discussion of these questions is a paper written by the American economists Modigliani and Miller

(Modigliani 1958). Their paper investigated whether a modified gearing ratio (meaning, a higher proportion of debt to equity finance) could achieve a lower overall cost of finance. Their conclusion was that markets will price the overall risk of an organisation accurately, and changing the proportion of debt to equity will not have an impact on the overall costs of finance. This paper by Modigliani and Miller suggests that Public Interest Companies cannot lower the overall costs of finance.

However, practical examples such as Glas Cymru and Nav Canada have demonstrated that debt financing alone can lower costs. How can this be the case?

The first part of the answer was highlighted by Modigliani and Miller themselves in a later amendment to their original publication that noted that greater value can be created through higher gearing when income tax is taken into account (Modigliani 1963). Debt and equity are treated in different ways for tax purposes; interest payments on debt are tax deductible, but dividends on equity are paid after tax.

This tax issue (along with other tax considerations discussed later) can have a significant impact on the costs of a single organisation, yet from a macro-economic viewpoint these tax issues offer no advantage. It would be foolish for the state to encourage the use of Public Interest Companies for the sole reason that they have lower costs, when it would be the state that bears the impact of these costs.

However, there is another instance when Modigliani and Miller's original hypothesis does not hold true. That is if the nature of the business environment changes. An example is when Consumer Service Corporations permit a fundamental change in the regulatory structure of an essential monopoly service. This can be achieved, as discussed earlier on pages 64-65, by the elimination of the natural pricing conflict inherent in shareholder-owned PLCs in particular circumstances. If the regulatory structure changes through the elimination of price regulation then, in effect, a new company emerges and added value has been created. The absence of regulatory risk can result in reduced prices for consumers or an increased asset valuation.

Case study 11: Network Rail

The privatisation of Railtrack was perhaps the most controversial of all the Conservative Government's privatisations. It was covered in the Railways Act of 1993, but it took until 1996 before Railtrack was sold off, the last part of the railway system to go.

The reasons for the controversy were well founded. Many details were rushed through in the haste to get the deal completed before the general election of 1997, and the company was sold for much less than its true value. In July 1999, the House of Commons Public Accounts Committee criticised the sale of Railtrack as 'poor value', with the taxpayer receiving less than £2 billion from the sale of shares, compared with the company's then current valuation of nearly £8 billion. In addition, Railtrack was a monopoly utility which carried out a key safety role. It was also massively dependent on government subsidy. There was a significant conflict of interests between the owners and the users of the company, and these conflicts played a key role in Railtrack's downfall.

In the years after the privatisation owners enjoyed a boost in the share price which rose from £3.80 to a high of £17.68 in November 1998. These profits were augmented by management's reluctance to invest resources in the long-term health of the network (by May 1997 Railtrack was £700 million behind on its rail investment and maintenance programme, described by the rail regulator as 'wholly unacceptable'). Instead, attention was focussed on making the most of Railtrack's significant property portfolio which offered more lucrative short-term potential for profits. This reluctance to invest in rail repairs was compounded by the engineering sub-contracting regime which left managers at Railtrack with little knowledge over what work was being carried out, and to what quality.

Any short-term increases in share price were undone when it became clear that Railtrack had neglected the core network at its peril following a series of crashes at Southall, Ladbroke Grove, Hatfield and Potters Bar. The share price fell back down to around £5, and it became clear that the company did not even have a proper asset register.

Rather than take the difficult long road of improving its core business, Railtrack had rightly considered that its best route to maintaining profits was to persuade government for ever-greater levels of subsidy. Much of this huge subsidy went through a revolving door at Railtrack, with shareholders benefiting from good dividend payments even when the company was in severe difficulty. Following a £1.5 billion subsidy from the Government, Railtrack's financial results for the year ending 31 March 2001 showed a pre-tax operating loss of £534 million, yet the company still paid a full-year dividend of 26.9p per share, which cost £138 million.

The crash at Hatfield in October 2000 signalled the end for Railtrack. In the panic in the aftermath of the crash Railtrack admitted that they had lost control of the network and put in place drastic speed restrictions across the network which brought the industry to its knees. In the end the Government refused to hand out any more subsidy and Railtrack was put into administration.

Shareholders were angry at this solution. They were threatened with bearing the financial risk of the company which they had always assumed the Government bore, not themselves. In the end, to avoid a lengthy court battle government compromised and gave shareholders nearly 90 per cent of the value of their shares when trading in the stock was suspended in 2001. The Government thus proved what the shareholders had suspected all along.

In January 2001, IPPR recommended that a Public Interest Company replace Railtrack. Government also decided that this was the best way forward for the company, and the Public Interest Company Network Rail came into existence in October 2002.

Network Rail is a 100 per cent debt-financed company limited by guarantee. The Government acts as risk-bearer through a series of contingent loans, and the company is expected to be governed by a 100 strong stakeholder membership, comprising of 40 industry members, 60 'public interest' members, and the Strategic Rail Authority – the Government's arms-length rail adviser. The Strategic Rail Authority plays a key role in the organisation, ensuring that public subsidy is spent wisely and that Network Rail helps implement the Government's strategic vision for the rail industry.

Network Rail is a better policy solution than Railtrack. However, it is not without its problems. For instance, although this report recommends that PICs are more suitable to inherently low risk businesses, Network Rail is anything but. Because of the dispute between Railtrack and the Government about administration, Network Rail was forced to buy the rail network blind. Moreover, Railtrack never carried out a proper audit of its assets. Also, during the period of administration, Network Rail's costs soared as maintenance decisions were carried out by engineers rather than managers. It is still struggling to get this spending under control.

The large amount of contingent loans – £21 billion – agreed by the Government mean that the Network Rail option is unlikely to be favoured again by the Treasury, not least because of the political wrangling over how this should be accounted for. Network Rail's borrowing was judged to be off the Government's balance sheet by the Office for National Statistics. However, Network Rail was judged to be a subsidiary of the Government's Strategic Rail Authority by the National Audit Office, who recommended that it should be included within the SRA's accounts. Government needs to develop alternatives to the either/or methodology for the national accounts to cope with these hybrid organisations and to avoid such conflicts.

Given that a range of stakeholders now govern Network Rail, the regulatory environment should also be changed. The rail regulator previously protected the public interest from the influence of private shareholders. Now the rail regulator faces competition in his protection of the public interest from Network Rail's public members. There is no need for the same kind of economic regulation to protect taxpayers from shareholders in the new Network Rail environment. As a result government should create a single strategic regulator for the railways by combining the functions of the SRA and the rail regulator (Grayling 2002).

Creating Network Rail was a brave and innovative policy decision by the Government. Although it may not serve as a model for future PICs, it is better suited to its purpose than Railtrack ever was.

What happens if a Public Interest Company goes bust?

Having the freedom to fail is one of the principles behind private companies. The fear of failure supposedly keeps companies lean and in theory ensures that only efficient companies survive.

However, a common criticism of PPPs generally and Public Interest Companies specifically is that they cannot be allowed to go bust because they deliver an essential public service. This criticism has led some to believe that PPPs - and especially the PFI - bear little or no risk.

Good PPPs do bear risk. If a PFI is designed where no risk is transferred there is likely to be no value for money reason to pursue the project. Just because ultimate risk is not transferred does not mean to say that other risks, such as completing construction to time and to budget, are not borne by the private sector.

The principle of contestability can provide solutions to what should happen if PPPs, including PICs, get into serious financial or performance difficulty. Contestability is a way of keeping public services accountable by demonstrating that where service providers are failing an alternative provider can be brought in to manage the service. Public Interest Companies will be more successful if it is made clear that they will be allowed to fail, and if they do, alternative management will be brought in. This will not always be easy for the Government; it risks both financial and political problems. However, if an organisation is heavily dependent on state subsidy and control it is unlikely to gain the benefits from being an independent 'private' sector operator. The key is to ensure that the delivery of what will often be a vital public service continues uninterrupted.

Tax and Public Interest Companies

We discussed earlier on page 75 how allowing for the different treatment of income tax for dividend payments and loan interest payments can appear to add value to a debt financed Public Interest Company. However, there are other tax arguments put forward for using Public Interest Companies.

For example, Public Interest Companies are used to run around 20 per cent of local authority leisure services, and a key driver is the significant tax advantages that come from this new status in the form of rate relief and the exemption of certain services from VAT. These financial benefits have been significant enough to provide short-term solutions to a need to reduce revenue expenditure on leisure services (4Ps 2001). There have also been recent claims that the 'not-for-profit PFI' being piloted in Argyle and Bute is seeking charitable status to gain similar tax advantages (*Public Private Finance* 2003).

However, tax advantages are a poor justification for using Public Interest Companies. Whilst it could be argued that the tax benefits of PIC leisure centres is a recognition for their wider community work, and as such represents indirect government subsidy of the sector, it could also be argued that the leisure centres are exploiting a legal tax loophole. As with all tax loopholes the Government is liable to change the rules and restore equity to the system, which could destroy any financial advantage of the projects.

Even where tax advantages are bestowed purposefully government should be conscious that there is no macro benefit from providing such tax advantages. Government simply suffers a loss in tax income, which it may have to make up from elsewhere in the tax system.

Case study 12: Not-for-profit PFIs

The PIC format can be used *within* other contractual relationships, for example in so-called 'not-for-profit PFIs'. These are similar to typical PFIs in that the public sector decides on outcomes and outputs, and then a private sector consortia designs, builds, finances and operates the scheme over 30 years or so, with annual payments based on the quality of the service delivered. The 'not-for-profit PFIs' differ in that the Special Purpose Vehicle (SPV - the company set up by the consortia to deliver the scheme) is organised as a type of Public Interest Company and financed through 100 per cent debt (rather than the typical mix in a PFI scheme of 90 per cent debt and 10 per cent equity). As such there are no profits to distribute to shareholders, hence 'not-for-profit'.

The policy advantage of these not-for-profit PFIs might not be immediately apparent. Indeed, the principle driver behind these schemes is politics. 'Profit' is still a dirty word for many when associated with public services, even where *for-profit* schemes have the potential to deliver better value for money than traditional procurement regimes. This antipathy to profits appears particularly acute in Scotland and Wales, and it is in a rebuild/refurbish project for 30 schools in the Scottish council of Argyle and Bute where the first modern not-for-profit PFI is being developed. The Scottish Liberal Democrats and the Scottish Nationalist Party have also both called for more 'not-for-profit' structures to be made available (Scottish National Party 2002; Liberal Democrat Party 1999).

But just how 'not-for-profit' are such schemes? Profits will still be made in these new PFIs, as it is even in traditional procurement options where the private sector is involved. Rather than profits being distributed direct from the special purpose vehicle, the contractors will receive their profits one step removed via subcontracts. Such a solution may appear more acceptable in areas where the typical PFI has been slow to take off. However, having been sold to a community as 'not-for-profit', there may be even greater public hostility if it is revealed that in fact companies will retain the same service delivery responsibilities and will make the same – or potentially even more – money out of the public sector.

If constituted carefully it is possible that a stakeholder-based special purpose vehicle could bring some practical advantages. Perhaps a special purpose vehicle governed in part by service users and local politicians might be more considerate in communicating with users and the wider community than those in typical PFIs. Where necessary, they might even make contract renegotiation less arduous. However, these benefits are not assured and such factors might be better fostered through good working relations between the commissioner and provider, regardless of organisational structures.

These types of PFIs also pose difficult questions regarding value for money, finance and risk. As 100 per cent debt-financed organisations they will have to deal with financial risk without the use of shareholders. There are potentially two ways of doing this, neither of which is entirely satisfactory. Firstly, lenders could be persuaded to bear the risk of the project, perhaps through subordinated debt; indeed this is the plan in Argyle and Bute. However, lenders usually *do not* bear risk and they may be reluctant to do so even if these PFIs only take place in less risky areas (as in education rather than technology PFIs), and even if there is minimal risk left within the SPV as a result of contracts placing this risk with sub-contractors. If lenders do bear risk they are likely to price this risk conservatively as a result of their inexperience so that they can give themselves room for manoeuvre; this is likely to result in poorer value for money for the public sector. Also, if lenders are being asked to shoulder risk through subordinated debt it is likely they will want substantial control over the activities of the organisation, reducing the influence of any stakeholder members, and potentially reducing the point of having a PIC structure at all.

A second way to deal with risk in not-for-profit PFIs is for the public sector to over-fund the project, thus helping the SPV build up surpluses which can act as an equity buffer. However, in effect this is a government guarantee, reducing the amount of risk transferred to the private sector. It is also cash inefficient from the Government's point of view. Because the public sector will pay more for the deal over its lifetime, this option again has serious value for money consequences.

Regardless of the method of dealing with risk, it is possible that not-for-profit PFIs will not reduce the costs of a scheme compared to a typical PFI, and if anything costs might actually increase.

However, one potential financial advantage of a not-for-profit PFI scheme is it could help reduce the short-term pressures that equity investors bring to a project. Using subordinated debt could result in a more public-sector-friendly long-term horizon.

Although there has been less success in school PFIs than elsewhere there are no obvious structural problems with contracting for the building and maintenance of a school building over a long period of time (Audit Scotland 2002; Audit Commission 2003). Unlike contracting for complex face-to-face public services it is difficult to argue that contracts are unable to specify the types of building outcomes required. As such there appears to be less justification for not-for-profit PFIs than other types of Public Interest Company. However, IPPR has long argued that there should be a greater diversity in PPP provision, and alternatives to school PFIs particular need to be developed (IPPR 2001). Although not conceptually perfect, not-for-profit PFIs could help provide such diversity, which in itself could help bring about an improved procurement regime.

The short-term influence of equity

Although equity is a tried and tested method of dealing with risk in private companies it has been criticised for its short-termism. As individuals we are constantly told that investing in the stock market is a long-term business, nonetheless, the horizons of institutional equity investors are notoriously short-term.

Because companies are so concerned about falls in their share price this can have a distorting short-term influence on business decisions (let us not forget that in equity based companies managers' bonus schemes are often linked solely to the level of share price). Equity investors will not be concerned about taking sensible business decisions for the long-term; they will be much concerned about the events of the next few weeks or months.

Typical private sector companies also suffer from these distorting pressures of equity. But in the invariably long-term low-yield public services, these issues are more acute.

Equity is designed to promoting entrepreneurial activity and extracts the last pound of value possible. But this activity comes at a cost. For stable or monopolistic situations there are few opportunities for such entrepreneurial activity, and few opportunities for the type of rapid growth that equity craves. For these types of environments equity might not only be inappropriate for the service, the service might be inappropriate for the needs of equity.

Interestingly, debt finance has a longer-term horizon than equity investment. This is because lenders are concerned that they have their principal (the amount they initially invested) at the end of the investment period. By using debt finance alone there is the potential for a better alignment of interests between the public interest and investor interest.

Case study 13: Local bus companies

The great majority of local bus services in the UK are privatised and deregulated. Local authorities have little control over what where and when bus services are provided, despite frequent subsidies to support routes that the bus companies see as uneconomical.

The Government has acknowledged this is a problem, and its Transport Act 2000 sought to increase the influence of local authorities over bus services through the use of 'quality partnerships' where the council improves road infrastructure in return for companies improving the quality of service, and 'quality contracts' where the council has a formal contract over service provision provided by private operators. IPPR has recommended that partnerships alone are unlikely to provide for improved levels of service, as demonstrated in London where a contracting system has helped bus use increase by 25 per cent between 1985-6 and 2001-2, compared to a fall outside London by 35 per cent (Department for Transport 2002; Grayling 2000).

However, there is an alternative model for bus services. In just 17 areas, the local authority owns the local bus company. Most are constituted as private limited companies where the council is the sole shareholder. These types of companies already come under our definition of Public Interest Companies. They can offer advantages of not seeing council subsidy being distributed to shareholders, they can help maintain a comprehensive network that covers both profitable and non-profitable routes, and they can help embed transport within other wider social policy goals.

There is an opportunity for bus companies to become more like the proposed arms-length housing companies. The local authority would reduce their stake but still maintain a substantial influence over bus services. A widened stakeholder membership might comprise the council, passengers and the wider community (including local businesses).

5. Conclusion

This report is a hard-headed examination of the 'new' concept of the Public Interest Company. It is written from a perspective of sympathetic scepticism.

In the search for better quality and more responsive public services government should have at its disposal a full range of organisational forms. Very often other factors, such as levels of funding or the organisation of staff will have a greater influence on service quality. But the basic organisational form of a public service can and often does play an important role.

The Government's choice of organisational forms for public services should be informed by practical possibilities, not dogma. Politics should focus on the *impacts* of any organisational change, not on ideological presumptions in favour or either public, private or hybrid ownership.

Attempting such an investigation of one type of organisational form will always be partial and problematic. These problems are compounded when discussing such a complex and fluid concept such as Public Interest Companies. In addition, this report has attempted to draw comparisons and learn lessons from a wide spectrum of public services; from the largest utilities to the smallest regeneration schemes; from key public services such as clinical care to obscure parts of the public service such as funding intermediary bodies. To claim a final or comprehensive account will be doomed to failure. Instead, this report hopes to have presented a rational case as to where, when and why PICs might have a role to play in delivering public services.

The conclusion is that although likely to be beset by complex problems, Public Interest Companies do have an important potential role to play in the public arena. In particular, there are four key areas where their use might be particularly appropriate:

- When contracting for complex public services where the public interest or issues such as safety are key, and where the usual reliance on a contract alone is unlikely to be enough to secure the public interest (for example, NHS foundation trusts).

- For local regeneration schemes or other areas of the public services where the key policy aim is to improve social capital and promote a greater involvement of the public in a particular service (for example, development trusts).

- For monopoly essential services where users are able to play an important governance role (for example, air traffic control and electricity distribution).

- For services where there is a significant element of public subsidy. For example, public transport. Where a service has both monopoly elements and high levels of public subsidy the case might be particularly strong (for example for Network Rail).

This list is clearly not exhaustive. One of the peculiar things about Public Interest Companies is there are many more organisations that have PIC features than one might first expect. Far from being a 'new' concept, they are in fact already widely used in various situations. Indeed, by promoting a degree of diversity in the delivery of public services, PICs might promote greater contestability and so help improve public services even when they do not appear to be the optimal solution.

This report has demonstrated that whilst PICs are potentially a useful organisational form, they are certainly not a panacea for the public services. Their use requires caution in two particularly complex areas: finance and governance. Government has not traditionally had much expertise in either of these and so particular caution must be exercised.

Many PICs will want to access the private finance markets to escape government borrowing restrictions. For taxpayer-funded services this logic is flawed. In any case, before any PIC raises private finance it should achieve clarity about how the financial risks of the organisation will be borne in the absence of shareholders. There are six principle ways in which such risk can be dealt with:

- lenders could bear the risks

- sufficient cash reserves can be built up over the short term to absorb expected future risks

- financial support can be obtained from taxypayers as a substitute for risk capital

- risks can be transferred on to the users of the service

- risks can be absorbed within the operational performance of the company

- risks can be externalised, through outsourced contracts or insurance

It may be that for taxpayer-funded PICs prudential borrowing frameworks offer a more sensible route of accessing private finance. It is also likely that PICs will be more suitable for sectors subject to relatively low risk. Government should find a new way to include hybrid structures like PICs and any contingent funding they rely on in the national accounts, without it being an either/or decision as to whether they are government liabilities.

It is clear that arguments will continue to rage over whether PICs provide better or worse forms of corporate governance than shareholder-owned companies. Whilst PICs can certainly provide greater openness, the Government will want to ensure that any stakeholder boards are capable of protecting their independence and of providing clear and, when necessary, tough guidance to directors about priorities. Meanwhile, presumptions that public involvement in corporate governance always leads to greater accountability need to be subject to rigorous analysis, as there may be alternative ways in which the responsiveness and accountability of public services can be improved. The public might be more interested in getting involved in the day-to-day management of services or in having their views taken into account, rather than providing arms-length corporate governance.

The success of Public Interest Companies will most likely not rest with technical questions about their suitability and rigour in particular situations. Politics alone is likely to drive their success or failure. As a 'new' political favourite, as a hybrid form that can be seen to embody the one-time fashionable 'third way' of the Labour Government, PICs are looked upon with both admiration and suspicion according to an individual's own view point. Such a situation is hardly novel; policy and politics are rightly interwoven. However, Public Interest Companies are in danger of becoming a new political fad. They should not be used for purely political considerations; some PICs, such as new 'not-for-profit' PFIs, might be used because they sound like more publicly acceptable forms of public private partnership, rather than because they offer substantial policy advantages.

PICs are only one solution to a range of public policy problems. Other organisational forms such as joint-ventures between the public and private sectors might achieve similar ends. However, based on the analysis contained in this report government should routinely consider using PICs alongside other organisational forms when deciding on the future of public services. If they do, and if they use them sparingly and wisely, then the modern day Public Interest Companies could last as long as some of the original PICs, the housing associations, which have survived for well over a century.

Endnotes

1 'There is little doubt that the voluntary sector – to use the most common term for the non-profit sector in the United Kingdom – is important' (Kendall 1993)

2 The Companies House online search engine allows you to discover the legal structure of most companies and other organisations: www.companieshouse.gov.uk/info

3 Glas Cymru's Articles of Association can be seen at www.glascymru. com/english/pdfenglish/documents/CorpGov.pdf.

4 Overall tenant satisfaction in housing associations was an average of 80 per cent, according to the 2002 Housing Corporation Performance indicators. Tenant satisfaction in local authority owned housing was an average of 77 per cent in 2001-2 according to the Audit Commission's Best Value Performance Indicator BVPI 74.

5 The NHS Bank has been created to reduce direct Whitehall control over some financial decisions in the NHS. Initially it has provided grants for improving productivity in the NHS, but in time it is likely to provide overdraft facilities for NHS Trusts and play a role in ensuring that capital decisions in the NHS are taken nearer the front line (NHS 2002).

88

References

4Ps (2001) *PFI and other PPPs in Local Government Leisure Services: State of the Market Report October 2001*

Ainger B (2000) 'Neighbourhood PPPs' in *New Economy* 7.3 IPPR

Anheier HK and Kendall J (2000) *Trust and voluntary organisations: Three theoretical approaches* London School of Economics Civil Society Working Paper 5

Audit Commission (2001) *Group dynamics: group structures and registered social landlords*

Audit Commission (2003) *PFI in schools: the quality and cost of buildings and services provided by early Private Finance Initiative schemes* January 2003

Audit Scotland (2002) *Taking the initiative: using PFI contracts to renew council schools* June 2002

Burns T (2003) *Why Glas Cymru was right for Wales* Comiston Lecture, 19.2.03

Brown G (2003) *A modern agenda for prosperity and social reform* Speech to the SMF at the Cass Business School, 3.2.03

Byatt I (2001) *Delivering Better Services for Citizens: A review of local government procurement in England* June 2001, DTLR

Byers S (2001) *Hansard* 23.10.01: Column: 195W

Cardew & Co (2002) *A call for an end to high electricity prices in Northern Ireland* Press release 12.6.02

Charity Commission (2003) *Choosing and preparing a governing document* CC22 www.charity-commission.gov.uk/publications/pdfs/cc22text.pdf

Corry D (2003) *The Regulatory State: Labour and the Utilities 1997-2002* IPPR

Corry D and Stoker G (2002) *New Localism: refashioning the centre-local relationship* New Local Government Network

Day G (2001) *New Paths for the Provision of Healthcare* Institute of Directors

Department for Transport (2002) *Transport statistics bulletin, A bulletin of public transport statistics: Great Britain: 2002 edition* Table 10 'local bus journeys by area' November 2002

Department of Health (2001) *Shifting the Balance of Power within the NHS: Securing delivery* July 2001

Department of Health (2002a) *Delivering the NHS Plan* April 2002

Department of Health (2002b) *A Guide to NHS Foundation Trusts* December 2002

Department of Health (2002c) *Reforming NHS Financial Flows: Introducing payment by results* October 2002

Director General for Electricity Supply (Northern Ireland) (2002) *An Independent Transmission System Operator for Northern Ireland: A Consultation Paper* March 2002

Duckworth S (2002) *The Structure and Financing of Registered Social Landlords* IPPR unpublished paper

Duggan M (2000) 'Hospital ownership and public medical spending' *The Quarterly Journal of Economics* November 2000

East End Life (2002) 'A radical approach to providing services' 5.8.02

Financial Times (2003) 'Council's chairman criticises plan for hospital boards' 1.3.03

Football Governance Research Centre (2002) *The State of the Game: The corporate governance of football clubs* for Supporters Direct

Franks J and Mayer C (2000) *Governance as a Source of Managerial Discipline* Prepared for the Company Law Review, Committee E on Corporate Governance, DTI, April 2000

Further Education Funding Council (1999) *Guide for further education governors*

Gibson-Smith C (2002) *Public Interest Companies and Risk* IPPR, July 2002 www.ippr.org

Glas Cymru (2001) *Annual General Meeting Corporate Governance Reference File* www.glascymru.com

Glas Cymru (2002) *Interim Results for the six months to 30 September 2002* Media release 14.11.02

Gollop R (2003) 'Modernisation: Fear of Flying' *Health Service Journal* 23.1.03

Gravatt J (2002) 'We must make it pay to enter the college market' *Times Educational Supplement* 22.3.02

Grayling T (2000) *Any more fares?* IPPR

Grayling T (2002) *Getting back on track* IPPR

Hackney Borough Council (2001) *Report of the Joint Team to Consider a New Body to Manage and Deliver Education Services in Hackney* October 2001

Ham C (1996) *Public, Private or Community: what next for the NHS?* Demos

Hansmann H (1996) *The Ownership of Enterprise* Harvard University Press

Harden I (1992) *The Contracting State* Open University Press

Hart OD (1995) *Firms, contracts and financial structures* Clarenden lectures, Clarenden Press

Hallgarten J (2000) *Parent's Exist OK?* IPPR

Hallgarten J (2003) 'The school to school market: supporting bottom-up innovation' *New Economy 10.1*

Hawksworth J (2000) 'Labour and Public Enterprise' in *New Economy 7.3* IPPR

Health Service Journal (2003a) 'Chiefs want fewer targets' 20.2.03

Health Service Journal (2003b) 'Foundations diluted to quieten MPs' 23.1.03

Hems L (2001) *The Organisational and Institutional Landscape of the UK Wider Nonprofit Sector* for Performance and Innovation Unit, The Cabinet Office. Centre for Voluntary Sector Policy, University College, London

Higgs D (2003) *Review of the role and effectiveness of non-executive directors January 2003* Department for Trade and Industry

HM Treasury (2002a) *The Role of the Voluntary and Community Sector in Service Delivery: A Cross Cutting Review*

HM Treasury (2002b) *Spending review: public service agreements 2002-2006*

Holtham G (1996) 'Water: Our Mutual Friend?' in *New Economy 3.4* IPPR

Holtham G (ed) (1998) *Freedom with Responsibility: Can we unshackle public enterprise?* IPPR

House of Commons Education and Employment Select Committee (1998) *Sixth Report Further Education* HC 264

House of Commons Environment, Transport and Regional Affairs Select Committee (2000) *The Proposed Public Private Partnership for National Air Traffic Services Limited*

House of Commons Treasury Select Committee (2003) *National Statistics: The classification of Network Rail*

Housing Corporation (1999) *Regulating Diversity: a discussion paper*

Housing Corporation, (2002) *Board Member Remuneration* Consultation paper

Housing Finance Corporation (2002) *Annual report 2001/2002*

IPPR (2001) *Building Better Partnerships: The Final Report of the Commission on Public Private Partnerships*

Jensen MC (1997) *Eclipse of the Public Corporation* Harvard Business School (revised 1997)

Kay J (2002) 'The Balance Sheet' in *Prospect* July

Kay J (2001) *Privatisation in the United Kingdom, 1979-1999* www.johnkay.com

Kelly G and Muers S (2002) *Creating Public Value: An analytical framework for public service reform* Prime Minister's Strategy Unit, Cabinet Office

Kendall J (2000) *The third sector and social care for older people in England: Towards an explanation of its contrasting contributions in residential care, domiciliary care and day care* Civil Society Working Paper 8, London School of Economics

Kendall J and Knapp M (1993) *Defining the Nonprofit Sector: The United Kingdom* The John Hopkins Institute

Kendall L and Lissauer R (2003 forthcoming) *The Future Healthworker* IPPR

La Porta R, Lopez-de-Silanes F and Shleifer A (1998) *Corporate Ownership around the World* October 1998

Leam D (2002) *All Aboard: Improving Public Service Accountability* Social Market Foundation

Liberal Democrat Party (1999) *LibDems call for radical changes to PFI as Bickerstaffe lays down challenge* Scottish Liberal Democrats Media release 15.2.99

Lloyd S (2001) *Growing the Public Sector: New Company Format Essential* PIC Group

McCallum D (2002) *Ownership, Governance and Rate Regulation in Essential Service Monopolies* IPPR www.ippr.org

Mayo E and Moore H (2001) *The Mutual State: How Local Communities can run Public Services* New Economics Foundation.

Milburn A (2002a) *Redefining the National Health Service* Speech to New Health Network 15.1.02

Milburn A (2002b) *NHS foundation trusts speech* 22.5.02

Modigliani F and Miller M (1958) 'The Cost of Capital, Corporate Finance, and the Theory of Investment' *American Economic Review* 48:261-297

Modigliani F and Miller M (1963) 'Corporate Taxes and the Cost of Capital: A Correction' *American Economic Review* 53: 433-492

Morse L (1997) 'Co-op Utilities, US style' in *New Economy* 4.4 IPPR

Mullins D and Riseborough M (2000) *What are housing associations becoming? Final Report of the changing with the Times project* Centre for Urban and Regional Studies, University of Birmingham

Murie A (2002) *Public Interest Companies and Public Private Partnerships: some questions from housing and regeneration activity* Unpublished paper, IPPR

National Audit Office (2002) *The Public Private Partnership for National Air Traffic Services* The Stationery Office

National Air Traffic Services (2001) *Safety and investment key to NATS' future says Airline Group* Media release 27.7.01

The National Council for Voluntary Organisations (2002) *Submission to the Treasury's cross cutting review of the role of the voluntary sector in public service delivery* January 2002

National Health Service (2002) *NHS Bank is latest move to decentralise power* Media release 17.5.02

New Economics Foundation (2002) *Network Rail could be worse than Enron* Media release 16.9.02

Norton EC and Staiger DO (1994) 'How Hospital Ownership Affects Access to Care for the Uninsured' *RAND Journal of Economics* 25: 171-185

Office of the Deputy Prime Minister (2003) *Sustainable Communities: Building for the future*

OFREG (2001) *Transmission and Distribution price control review for Northern Ireland Electricity* November 2001

Palmer K (2003) *Foundation Trusts and the New Architecture of the NHS* Cambridge Economic Policy Associates Ltd

Performance and Innovation Unit (2001) *Voluntary Sector Review: Charitable Status*

PricewaterhouseCoopers Corporate Finance (2002) *Financing and Risk Issues Associated with Not-for-profit models applied to UK Public Private Partnerships* IPPR www.ippr.org

Public Management Foundation (2001) *The Case for a Public Interest Company: A new Form of Enterprise for Public Service Delivery*

Public Finance (2003) 'Hopes of wider borrowing powers dashed by Prescott's "grand plan"' 7.7.03

Public Private Finance (2003) 'Tax reprieve for not-for-profit PPPs' December 2002/January 2003

Salamon LM and Anheier HK (eds) (1997) *Defining the Nonprofit Sector: A Cross-National Analysis* Manchester University Press

Salamon LM (1992) *America's Nonprofit Sector: A Primer* Foundation Centre

Scottish National Party (2002) *The Scottish Trust for Public Investment* Briefing paper

Standard Life (2002) *Standard Life members to vote on regulation changes* Media release 27.3.02

Steele J and Corrigan P (2001) *What Makes a Public Service Public?* Public Management Foundation, London

Stones C (2001) *Changes in the Pipeline? Economic and Public Policy Implications of Water Industry Restructuring* Social Market Foundation

Strategy Unit (2002) *Private Action Public Benefit* Prime Minister's Strategy Unit, Cabinet Office

Transport for London (2001) *Summary of PPP Performance Regime* Briefing document

Warren RC (2000) *Corporate Governance and Accountability* Liverpool Academic Press

Weisbod B (ed) (1999) *To Profit or Not To Profit* Cambridge University Press

Westall A (2001) *Value-Led Market-Driven: Social Enterprise Solutions to Public Policy Goals* IPPR

Whitehead C (1999) *The Provision of Finance for Social Housing: the UK Experience* London School of Economics